RACISM OR ATTITUDE?

The Ongoing Struggle for Black Liberation and Self-Esteem

RACISM OR ATTITUDE?

The Ongoing Struggle for Black Liberation and Self-Esteem

JAMES L. ROBINSON, Ph. D.

Foreword by
Mitchell F. Rice, Ph. D.

INSIGHT BOOKS

Plenum Press • New York and London

Library of Congress Cataloging-in-Publication Data

Robinson, James L.
    Racism or attitude? : the ongoing struggle for Black liberation
and self-esteem / James L. Robinson ; foreword by Mitchell F. Rice.
        p.   cm.
    Includes bibliographical references and index.
    ISBN 0-306-44945-5
    1. Afro-Americans--Race identity.   2. United States--Race
relations.   I. Title.
E185.625.R56   1995
305.896'073--dc20   95-2369
                                                                  CIP

ISBN 0-306-44945-5

© 1995 James L. Robinson
Insight Books is a Division of Plenum Publishing Corporation
233 Spring Street, New York, N.Y. 10013-1578

An Insight Book

10 9 8 7 6 5 4 3 2 1

Printed in the United States of America

Foreword

James Robinson has written a book that discusses contemporary black attitudes and public policy in America. He challenges many of the major assumptions made by black leaders and other liberal thinkers regarding the role that racism and discrimination play in keeping many African Americans from achieving success in America. He argues that though racism has been detrimental to blacks in America, it is no longer racism that is limiting black progress. What is limiting black progress is the belief that blacks have about racism, namely, the belief that racism keeps blacks from achieving.

Dr. Robinson argues that this belief in racism's power is a self-fulfilling prophecy and that it stops many African Americans from even trying to succeed. Throughout the book he cites examples of how various black leaders have used racism as an excuse for explaining some of the pathos found in ghetto life.

The analyses in his book combine social science research, political essay, and commentary in an attempt to answer the following questions: Why is it that some African Americans are prospering and doing better than ever before while others (too many) are not? And what needs to be done so that all African Americans can share in the American dream?

Although Dr. Robinson believes that racism and discrimination should be vigorously fought at every turn, he does not feel that this approach will lead to the social and economic liberation of African Americans. Real liberation, he argues, will occur only when black attitudes about race change, for if African Americans believe that they are destined to fail because they are black, then that belief becomes the working assumption on which they base their actions.

Dr. Robinson criticizes those successful blacks who promote the notion that less successful blacks have failed because of their color. He believes that race is used as an excuse for a ghetto lifestyle. Dr. Robinson strongly challenges the message that racism is the main obstacle to black progress.

Whether one agrees or disagrees with this book, it is controversial and it will certainly begin a dialogue that can only be healthy. It is hoped that out of needed dialogue will come some changes in attitudes and perspectives.

MITCHELL F. RICE, PH.D.

Professor of Political Science and
Public Administration
Louisiana State University
Baton Rouge, Louisiana

Acknowledgments

I first want to acknowledge the influence of William Julius Wilson's book *The Declining Significance of Race*, which I read while teaching at Rutgers University in 1981. It started me thinking about racism in an entirely different way. I also wish to thank some of the black conservative thinkers who were brave enough to argue a different point of view, even though they knew that they would be severely criticized by many in the black community.

I owe special thanks to my agent, Gerry Wallerstein, who received an early proposal and saw merit in it. She stuck with me over several drafts of the book and always gave helpful suggestions. I would also like to thank my editor, Frank Darmstadt, who has been very helpful and supportive. He has made editorial suggestions that have proven to be very useful in fully developing my material. He has also been extremely flexible in terms of deadlines, which he graciously extended.

Finally, I want to thank my wife, Adriene, for her readings and helpful suggestions. She made editorial corrections that were invaluable in completing my project.

Contents

RACISM OR ATTITUDE?

The Ongoing Struggle for Black Liberation and Self-Esteem

Introduction

In 1995 it can be said that, for African Americans, "it is the best of times, it is the worst of times," to paraphrase Charles Dickens. For many African Americans things are better than ever before. But for too many others, times couldn't be worse. This book is dedicated to analyzing why so many African Americans live more dysfunctional lifestyles today then thirty or forty years ago. Consider the following statistics.

In 1965, Daniel P. Moynihan shocked America when he issued a policy paper, *The Negro Family: The Case for National Action* (now known as the "Moynihan Report"), stating that 25 percent of all black families were female-headed.[1] Yet by 1980, according to the 1980 U.S. census, that figure had risen to 43 percent, and the 1990 U.S. census shows the number to be over 50 percent.[2] Moynihan's report deplored the fact that one-quarter of all black births were out of wedlock. However, in 1980 census data show these births had risen to 50 percent and 1990 census data has them at a staggering 63.7 percent.[3] The 1990 U.S. Department of Justice *Uniform Crime Reports* showed African Americans made up 49 percent of all inmates in state and federal prisons.[4] In fact, if

1

these statistics are compared with data in the 1993 *U.S. Statistical Abstracts*, one finds as many blacks in correctional facilities as in colleges.[5]

The 1990 census reported that 45 percent of all black children lived in families with incomes below the poverty line.[6] But these same data show that these children are overwhelmingly in female-dominated households, which are almost guaranteed to have low income. William Julius Wilson, a prominent black sociologist at the University of Chicago, argues in his book *The Truly Disadvantaged* that "economic hardship has become almost synonymous with black female-headed families. . . . Even if a female householder [white or black] is employed full-time, her earnings are usually substantially less than that [sic] of a male worker and are not likely to be supplemented with income from a second full-time employed member of the household."[7]

Aggregate black income continues to lag seriously behind that of whites. In 1990 the median income for white households was $31,435; for black households it was $19,758. Yet, for two-earner families, black income was 88 percent of that of similar white families.[8] And Sam Roberts also reported in *Who We Are* that some blacks had actually reached income parity with whites in certain areas of the United States. Roberts used the 1990 census data to substantiate his findings. Roberts states, "The median income of black households in Queens [New York] adjusted for inflation, rose in a decade by 31 percent, compared to an increase of 19 percent for white households. Even more impressive than the rate was the result. In 1980 the census found that the black household median income was 9.5 percent less than it was for whites. By 1990 the disparity had shrunk to a statistically insignificant .2 percent."[9]

According to U.S. census figures, from 1967 to 1991 the proportion of black households earning $50,000 or more a year rose from 5.3 to 12.1 percent. The proportion earning $100,000 and up in those same years more than doubled, from 0.5 percent to 1.2 percent.[10] While the figures lagged behind those for whites, with 27.5 percent earning $50,000 or more in 1991, and 4.8 percent earning $100,000 or more, these numbers do show substantial growth for the black middle class.[11] It is equally clear that the living standards of poor blacks have deteriorated relative to wealthy blacks, relative to poor whites, and even absolutely. As Thomas and Mary Edsalls documented in *Chain Reaction*, "From 1973 to 1987 families in the bottom quintile of the black income distribution became 18 percent poorer in constant dollars— as against a smaller loss of 7 percent for families in the bottom quintile of the white distribution. In the same period, families in the top quintile of the black distribution gained 33 percent."[12] In other words, the black middle class became richer and poor blacks became even poorer. Joseph Perkins, a black reporter for the *San Diego Union*, wrote on October 2, 1990, that "the best gauge of the overall status of black America is the extent of gains by the majority of black population: the number of college-educated blacks, the size of the black middle-class, the rate of black employment growth, the growth of the black business sector, and the numbers of blacks in the professions. By these important measures of progress, blacks fared extremely well during the last decade [1980s]."[13]

As can be seen, the above statistics present a disturbing paradox: They show two separate black communities, with one achieving successes never imagined just a few years ago and the other sinking into greater desperation. The achievers: In 1992, the first African American woman, Carol Moseley Braun from Illinois, was elected to the United States Senate, and the governor of Virginia, L. Douglas Wilder, was an African American, which is particularly ironic since Virginia was the state where the first African slaves landed in 1619. In business, politics, sports, and entertainment, African Americans are breaking new ground in achievement. Yet, in other areas, such as crime, ghetto living conditions, and family life, some African Americans are achieving new lows.

The 1990 census data show that the unemployment rate of blacks is the same as it was in 1960, more than twice that of whites. The same data report that a black child is about three times as likely to be born into poverty; more than half of all black children live in single-parent families, and only one-sixth of white children do.[14] The Department of Justice *Uniform Crime Reports* indicate a black man is six times as likely as a white man to be murdered, and his murderer is likely to be black. FBI 1994 crime statistics found more blacks being killed in our streets by each other than black servicemen killed during the entire Vietnam war.[15] And most significantly, since the 1970s these racial statistics have all grown or held steady.[16]

Many African Americans blame white racism for these negatives. They argue that it is continued racial discrimination which perpetuates ghetto lifestyles. This position is particularly championed by the National Urban League, the National Association for the Advancement of Colored People (NAACP), and other civil rights organizations. Their argument is that white racism has kept blacks down in the past and is continuing to do so today. This position has remained largely unchallenged, even though it runs counter to a great deal of evidence. While it is certainly true that racism played its part historically to keep African Americans down, it is not clear that racism and discrimination are the sole culprits today. If white racism and discrimination are the sole culprits, why are fewer black males with their families today than in 1955? In 1955, by every sociological measure, racism and discrimination were worse in America.[17] For research discussing changing white attitudes about blacks see "Racial Ambivalence and American Value Conflict: Correlational and Priming Studies of Dual Cognitive Structures" by Irwin Katz and R. Glen Hass (*Journal of Personality and Social Psychology*, 1988), which discusses a change in white racial attitudes and affirms less prejudiced beliefs about blacks, and James R. Kluegel's study "Trends in Whites' Explanations of the Black–White Gap in Socioeconomic Status, 1977–1989" (*American Sociological Review*, August 1990), which reports a significant decline over the years in the percentage of whites attributing the gap to the innate inferiority of blacks. These two studies are not exhaustive, but they are representative of studies which show a change in white attitudes. Other empirical evidence of this change in white attitudes is the explosion of black elected officials, many of whom have been elected in areas where blacks are not in a majority, for example, Los Angeles (black mayor Thomas Bradley), New York City (black mayor David Dinkins), Illinois (black woman senator Carol Moseley Braun), Virginia (black governor Douglas Wilder), and the list goes on.

Can racism be blamed for sending so many young black men into federal and state prisons? While the criminal justice system appears to be somewhat racially biased in its sentencing practices, Wilson cites studies in *The Declining Significance of Race* which show that the number of African Americans incarcerated for serious crimes such as murder, assault, rape, and armed robbery is proportionate to the reporting of those crimes.[18] In other words, large numbers of serious crimes are reported by African Americans in their communities. The perpetrators of those crimes tend to be largely African Americans; as a result, they are incarcerated.[19] Rather than analyze the question of whether African

Americans are unfairly treated in the criminal justice system, a more probing question would be why so many African Americans commit crimes. Is it the fault of the criminal justice system that so many African Americans are in prison, or is it the fault of those who commit the crimes? Also, if racial discrimination in employment, housing, and the way blacks are treated in the criminal justice system are to be blamed for a high crime rate in black ghettos, why wasn't crime worse back in the 1930s, 1940s, and 1950s, when African Americans were not only being severely discriminated against but were also being systematically and publicly lynched?

For example, Wilson notes that at the turn of the twentieth century as many as 161 African Americans were lynched in one year in the United States.[20] Lynchings were quite common right up to the 1950s and were done, according to Glazer and Moynihan's *Beyond the Melting Pot*, to "control Negroes." I agree with Wilson when he says there is no parallel between the racism practiced today and the violent racial attacks and antagonisms of earlier years.[21] One need only read Alan Grimshaws's accounts in his book *A History of Racial Conflict in America*, to know that racial attacks against blacks were a severe problem.[22]

This book will try to answer the following questions: If actual racism and racial oppression of blacks are less today than forty or fifty years ago, why are conditions in the black community so much worse, as has been pointed out in the above statistics? Why are there *more* out-of-wedlock births to black women today (63.7 percent) than in 1965, when Moynihan reported (25 percent)? Why are black-on-black crime statistics going up every year according to the FBI?[23] And why have some blacks been able to grab hold of the brass ring of success while others have not?

One of the answers to the above questions is surprising because it involves the success of the civil rights movement of the 1950s and 1960s. Ironically, much of the dysfunction we see in today's ghettos was created, in part, by this success. The civil rights movement was largely a black middle-class movement. In the South, it was pushed forward by middle-class black college students and black churches.[24] The major beneficiaries were and are middle-class African Americans who gained important freedoms which allowed them greater socioeconomic mobility.[25] The movement liberated middle-class African Americans from the ghetto by creating more housing mobility, and middle-class blacks moved from the inner cities to the suburbs. When these middle-class blacks left the older ghettos en masse, they left behind the blacks who were the poorest and least educated.[26]

Once the word *ghetto* meant just that, a walled part of a city where all African Americans, like the Jews of Warsaw and Hungary in 1939, were confined. Black doctors, lawyers, teachers, and other professionals lived in the ghetto.[27] They had no choice. They sent their children to the same schools as poorer blacks, shopped in the same stores, and used the same recreational facilities. These middle-class African Americans provided an important degree of political and social stability. They provided role models for other blacks who might strive for a middle-class lifestyle.[28]

However, the success of the civil rights movement in removing restrictive covenants and other forms of housing discrimination allowed these professional and other middle-class blacks to leave, thus creating today's ghetto. More and more blacks are leaving the inner cities and moving to the suburbs. According to U.S. census data, the black population in the suburbs more than doubled between 1960 and

1980, going from 2.8 million to 6.2 million.[29] Cities like Chicago lost 115,000 blacks during the 1980s, but Chicago's suburbs gained 103,000 blacks.[30] In places like Washington, D.C., the nation's capital, blacks in the middle class live in suburbs like Prince Georges County, Maryland. Unlike anytime before, today's ghetto is populated by the most disadvantaged segment of the African American community. This group is characterized by individuals who lack training and skills. They are the hard-core unemployed, and some have never held jobs. Wilson describes this group as "individuals who are engaged in street crime and other forms of aberrant behavior, and families that experience long term spells of poverty and/or welfare dependency. These are the populations to which I refer when I speak of the *underclass*."[31]

This book will challenge the popular and politically correct position that the condition that a significant number of African Americans find themselves in today is due to racism and discrimination. On the contrary, I argue that it is not racism, but racism's demise, that is responsible for creating a black underclass. I also argue that macroeconomics, not racism, has played a significant part in creating a somewhat permanent underclass by eliminating many of the manufacturing jobs that a previous generation of blacks could obtain. My father, an uneducated black farm worker from rural Texas, was able to buy homes and raise and provide for his family by working in one of those well-paying manufacturing jobs.

I also think the so-called black underclass has to accept some responsibility for ghetto conditions. Too often, conditions in the ghetto are blamed on everyone except those who live there. Blaming others for one's condition is making oneself a victim, and victims give up much of their personal power to effect change. For years, too many years, African Americans have waited for something to happen, for the government to give us our "forty acres and a mule." (Supposedly to entice black ex-slaves to fight for the Union, Abraham Lincoln promised to give them forty acres and a mule when the war was over.) We never got those forty acres or the mule, and I think the days of massive government action on behalf of blacks are over. Neither the resources nor the political climate exist today for that kind of intervention.

Yet there are opportunities for African Americans to prosper in America, and many blacks have taken advantage of them. As I stated earlier, about 12.1 percent of all black families earn $50,000 or more, and this is the highest percentage ever recorded. Current census data also show that disparities between white and black income narrow when factors like geographic region, education, and occupation are taken into account.[32] Contrary to the civil rights community's contention, not all blacks are poor and down and out. Bart Landry, a professor at the University of Maryland, predicts that if present trends continue, the black middle class might be as large in percentage terms for blacks as the white middle class is for whites.[33] But seldom does one hear such optimism reported in the media. As Milton D. Morris, former director of research at the Joint Center for Political Studies (a black think tank in Washington, D.C.), stated, "There is a story to be told. And it is a story of the success of the revolution of the last 20 years. It's almost as if we would rather not focus on that side of the picture, because after all, the glass is half-empty. Many people still perceive the results as very, very tenuous. It's like, 'Yes there are these things, but we really don't believe it's for real; we can't take it too seriously because it could disappear any minute.' But those successes, they're there. They're real. They ought to inspire us [blacks]."[34]

A 1991 study by the Urban Institute (a Washington, D.C., think tank) directly challenges the notion of widespread hiring discrimination against blacks in employment. In this study the institute hired twenty male college students (ten white and ten black) and carefully matched them in black–white pairs so that each had virtually identical skills, résumés, appearance, and demeanor. They were then sent out to Washington, D.C., and Chicago to apply for a range of jobs advertised in the newspapers. Their progress was monitored not only to see whether one received a job offer or not but also to examine each stage of the application process in order to check for racial bias.

According to the institute's results, "In 80 percent of the job searches, both the white and the black applicants were offered equivalent jobs. In 15 percent, the white received a job offer over the black; in 5 percent, the black got the job, and the white didn't." The report contained other encouraging news. For example, there was no evidence that racial discrimination against blacks occurred more often in suburban and predominantly white neighborhoods than in the inner city. In Chicago, blacks were actually more likely than whites to receive favorable treatment in the early stages of job application.[35]

The Urban Institute's report presents a story that has received little attention in civil rights circles. One has to wonder why. Could it be that the report's conclusions do not further the "politically correct" idea that racism is rampant in hiring, and that blacks are being victimized by it? The institute concluded that 73 percent of the job searches were nondiscriminatory, while 27 percent had some discrimination either in hiring or in the application process. Discrimination in 27 percent of the job searches is still too high, but the study does show that in the overwhelming majority of hiring decisions, race was not a factor. Ironically, the above data on hiring substantiate earlier data which describe the increase of the black middle class. Obviously some blacks are getting well-paying jobs, making money, and generally progressing in America.

I do not discount a continuing pattern of racism in America. Throughout this book I argue that racism is still a problem. It has been here since the first blacks stepped off the boat, as slaves, in Virginia in 1619. However, racism in America has undergone a number of permutations from the violent lynchings of forty years ago to its more subtle forms today. And while white racism remains a problem, not only for African Americans but for other groups as well, I argue that an even more serious problem is black attitudes about race. For many blacks, the cry of racism has become almost a crutch to be used when trying to explain a growing black underclass. Civil rights groups use this term to explain away rising crime statistics, family demise, and lower-class black lifestyles.

William Raspberry, a widely read black *Washington Post* journalist, has written that present-day black attitudes about racism are based in myth. He quickly points out that most myths are based on actual experiences and can make a profound difference in group outcome. Raspberry says he came to this conclusion from a letter he received from one of his readers, a Virginia educator named Mary Pringle. He quotes Pringle, who said that "racism is reality, but it has been overcome by many and given way to opportunity and success. Those who have overcome it, she argued, have been moved by different myths: myths that paint them as destined for success rather than doomed to failure, myths that lead them to see themselves as members of a special group capable of overcoming all odds. That is the kind of myth that blacks need to cultivate, she said."[36] Raspberry goes on to say that though racism is founded in reality, it is a particularly destructive myth because it gives greater power to the odds against success than actually exist. This makes it harder for those who believe in this myth even to try to succeed. He believes that what the black community needs is a "stronger more powerful myth that is constructive and evokes a sense of identity and energy to move ahead."[37]

Raspberry's point is that people act on what they believe. He talks about black youngsters believing in the myth that blacks are gifted athletes, particularly in basketball, which moves them to practice shooting balls for hours on end; they are rewarded with skills in that area. Asian kids are told that they have special talents in math and science, and so they spend hours studying these subjects and are rewarded for their hard work. Jewish kids believe they are gifted in writing and so spend additional time acquiring writing skills, thus proving the belief to be true. Positive beliefs or myths, as Raspberry calls them, are good and empower, but negative beliefs are destructive. Success or failure in any enterprise is due, in large part, to the beliefs we bring with us when we step to the table. If African Americans believe that they cannot succeed until white people love them, then they will not succeed because they have given the power of success to someone outside themselves.

If racism is the reason so many blacks are poor, how does one explain poor whites? While the percentages of black poor are greater, this still does not explain Appalachia, where white poverty is persistent and pernicious. These whites don't suffer from white racism and, in fact, can live, work, and go anywhere they please. I discuss the issue of racism in more detail in Chapter 1.

In this book I have chosen to use the terms *black* and

African American interchangeably, although I do have a preference for the word *black* in describing people of African ancestry. I like to use *black* because it helped me and, I suspect, many other blacks in my generation (1960s) overcome the negative connotation the word had when describing my race. Forty years ago very few "African Americans" wanted to be "black." But during the late 1960s this all changed with the "black power" movement. *Black* became the word of choice when speaking about "blacks" and brought a kinship, a togetherness, among those with the darkest to the lightest skin color. Using the word *black* in a positive manner helps counter the negative Eurocentric uses of *black*. Words like *blackmail, blackjack,* and *blacklisted* are only a few of the negative examples. For people of color to accept *black* as a positive description of themselves helps them to heal the negative psycholinguistic connotations of the word (psycholinguistics is the study of how language and word usage affect beliefs).

In Chapter 1, "Race Thinking," I discuss the origins of black attitudes about race. I point out what the benefits are for African Americans who believe racism is to blame for their problems.

Chapter 2, "Race or Class? A Classic Debate," is a discussion of social class and race. It is a detailed analysis of contradictions between race and class thinking. Also discussed is why African Americans fear being called middle class.

Chapter 3, "The Price of Affirmative Action," is a discussion of affirmative action, highlighting both good and bad aspects. I argue that affirmative action exacts a price from its beneficiaries by continuing the feeling of inferiority.

In Chapter 4, "Crime and Punishment," I discuss issues of law enforcement in the black community. There is a love–

hate relationship with the police in the ghetto. What are the solutions to the rising black crime rate?

Chapter 5, "Blacks, Jews, Koreans, and Hispanics in the Promised Land," explores the relationship between blacks, Jews, and other ethnic groups in America. Blacks and Jews have a love–hate relationship but are drawn together by their mutual interest in fighting racism and anti-Semitism. I also discuss the reasons that blacks resent Asian merchants in their neighborhoods and the up-and-coming power struggle blacks are going to have with an ever-increasing Hispanic presence in the ghetto.

Chapter 6, "Welfare Dependency," discusses and analyzes black dependence on outside forces to solve problems. Welfare dependency and solutions are discussed as well as black attitudes about dependence on the government to solve problems.

Chapter 7, "The Declining Significance of Integration," explores the demise of integration as a viable goal for the black community. Black attitudes toward an integrated society are only lukewarm.

Chapter 8, "Black Empowerment," argues that African Americans should change their attitudes about racism and victimhood. Examples are given of African Americans taking charge of negative environments and improving them.

Chapter 9, "Conclusion," discusses a concept called *racial healing*. This chapter explores the need for black folks to be completely honest with themselves, even at the risk of suffering some pain. The reality of modern-day American life is that racism does less to keep blacks impoverished than do their beliefs about racism.

CHAPTER ONE

Race Thinking

The famous black writer James Baldwin once wrote that the worst thing about his father was not that white people called him (the father) a nigger, but that he believed it. Despite the very serious recent recession, 1990 census tract data show that many blacks are better off today than ever before. Yet, when one listens to black leadership, it would appear that things are worse for all blacks. I believe the reason for this pessimism is twofold: One reason is political and the other is guilt. The political reason that black leadership seldom speaks about the progress many blacks have made is their fear that they might lose federal programs if whites believe blacks are not so badly off after all. These leaders are still caught up in the belief that somehow the federal government will spend large amounts of money on race-specific programs. The second reason we never hear anything good about black progress is guilt. I believe many middle-class blacks feel guilty about being better off. They feel that somehow their living a better life contradicts the suffering of less-well-off African Americans. Every time I hear middle-class black spokespeople say that things have not improved for blacks, what they mean is others, not themselves.

The 1980 and 1990 census data discussed in the previous chapter show clearly that black income gains are most prevalent among those who already had higher incomes to start. The Thomas and Mary Edsalls data, previously cited, show that from 1973 to 1987 blacks in the lowest income brackets became 18 percent poorer, yet during the same period blacks in the highest income brackets became 33 percent richer. While these data show a definite need for improvement among the lower-income blacks, there is no reason for black leadership to say there is no improvement for any blacks. But when asked why one-third of blacks are doing so poorly, black leaders say the reason is continuing white racism in America. They tend to ignore other reasons like destructive ghetto lifestyles or changes in the global economy. Why this obsession with racism? Is racism a myth, as William Raspberry called it in his quote in the previous chapter? I agree with Raspberry that racism has taken on mythological qualities for many black people, but the belief in racism also has certain functional attributes which Raspberry does not discuss. I think that functionally, the belief in "racism" as the main obstacle to black progress binds all African Americans together in a way that socioeconomic status does not. The belief in "racism" as a major source of black woes has come to define blackness in a way that allows all black people, from Oprah Winfrey to the lowest black person on the totem pole, to feel a sense of unity. "No matter how successful I become," says the middle-class black, "I can still say to my lower-class black brother, 'Hey, I'm not doing so good; I am still suffering because I am black.'" But the idea that being black means that all blacks suffer equally is to deny some of the real struggles and challenges facing inner-city poor blacks. It is not true that the blacks in the suburbs, making

$50,000 a year, with two cars in the garage, are suffering as are their ghetto counterparts in the cities.

The term *racism* was not commonly used in social science or American public life until the 1960s. *Racism* does not appear, for example, in the Swedish economist Gunnar Myrdal's classic 1944 study, *American Race Relations: An American Dilemma*. But even when the term was not directly used, it is still possible to determine that there was a prevailing understanding of racial oppression. In the 1940s *racism* referred to an ideology, an explicit system of beliefs postulating the superiority of whites based on the inherent, biological inferiority of the colored races. Bob Blauner published an article in the January 1993 *Current* called "Language of Race: Talking Past One Another," in which he states, "Ideological racism was particularly associated with the belief systems of the Deep South and was originally devised as a rationale for slavery. Theories of white supremacy, particularly in their biological versions, lost much of their legitimacy after the Second World War due to their association with Nazism." In recent years cultural explanations of "inferiority" are heard more commonly than biological ones, which today are associated with such extremist "hate groups" as the Ku Klux Klan and the White Aryan Brotherhood.[1]

According to Blauner, by the 1950s and early 1960s, with ideological racism discredited, the focus shifted to a more discrete approach to racially invidious attitudes and behavior, expressed in the model of prejudice and discrimination. *Prejudice* referred (and still does) to hostile feelings and beliefs about racial minorities and to the web of stereotypes justifying such negative attitudes. *Discrimination* referred to actions meant to harm the members of a racial minority group. The logic of this model was that racism implied a double standard, that is, treating a person of color differently—in mind or action—than one would a member of the majority group. By the mid-1960s the terms *prejudice* and *discrimination* and the implicit model of racial causation implied by them were seen as too weak to explain the sweep of racial conflict and change, too limited in their analytical power, and, for some critics, too individualistic in their assumptions. Their original meanings tended to be absorbed by the new, more encompassing idea of racism. During the 1960s the referents of racial oppression moved from individual actions and beliefs to group and institutional processes, from subjective ideas to "objective" structures or results. Instead of intent, there was now an emphasis on process: those more objective social processes of exclusion, exploitation, and discrimination that led to a racially stratified society.

The most notable of these new definitions was "institutional racism." In their 1967 book *Black Power*, Stokely Carmichael and Charles Hamilton stressed how institutional racism was different and more fundamental than individual racism. Racism, in this view, was built into society and scarcely required prejudicial attitudes to maintain racial oppression. This understanding of racism as pervasive and institutionalized spread from relatively narrow "movement" and academic circles to the larger public, with the appearance in 1968 of the report of the commission on the urban riots appointed by President Lyndon Johnson and chaired by Illinois Governor Otto Kerner. The Kerner Commission identified "white racism" as a prime reality of American society and as the major underlying cause of ghetto unrest. America, in this view, was moving toward two societies, one white and one black (it is not clear where other racial minorities fit in). Although its recommendations were never acted on politically, the report legitimized the term *white racism* among politicians and opinion leaders as a key to analyzing racial inequality in America.

Another definition of racism, which I would call *racism as atmosphere*, also emerged in the 1960s and 1970s. This is the idea that an organization or an environment may be racist because its implicit, unconscious structures are devised for the use and comfort of white people, with the result that people of other races do not feel at home in such settings. Last, perhaps the most radical definition of all was the concept of *racism as result*. In this sense, an institution or an occupation is racist simply because racial minorities are underrepresented in numbers or in positions of prestige and authority.

These theoretical concepts of racism were developed mainly by academicians and political activists over the years. In his book *The American Prospect*, Bob Blauner has a very good discussion of the history of racism as a world concept. I believe, however, that "racism," as a concept, serves a more psychological purpose for both lower- and middle-class blacks. Middle-class blacks use "racism" to absolve their guilt by saying how profoundly they are affected by it. And lower-class blacks use "racism" as an excuse for not trying harder or for giving up trying at all. The term *racism* also has a certain power for the person using it. It worked well for aspiring Supreme Court Justice Clarence Thomas during his judicial confirmation hearings. White liberal Senators were visibly shaken when Judge Thomas told them they were conducting a "high-tech lynching" because he was an "uppity black." What did Clarence Thomas do? He played the "race card." He did what African Americans do all the time; he exercised his moral superiority as a black man. He reminded the Senators that he was, after all, a black man and that they were white males, who at the very least had some guilt to bear vis-à-vis black men.

Racism has become a term that all African Americans can use to explain whatever problems they confront because it absolves them of personal responsibility. If a black man deserts his family, it's due to racism. If a black college student has poor grades, it is because his white professors are racists. All problems are seen as coming from outside the self. During the 1960s black prison inmates called themselves political prisoners. They accepted no personal responsibility for their actions.

The real issues behind a black man's leaving his family or the college student's failures might require a very different explanation from racism. One possible reason black men leave their families may be that they feel they can't provide their families with the things they need. Unemployment is one contributing reason why poor families break apart, both white and black. As was stated earlier, if racism is the only culprit in creating fatherless black families, then why are there more of these families today than during the 1950s, when racism was worse?

The black family has been under siege for over thirty years, and its decline appears to be due, in part, to cultural and social dynamics that occurred when blacks left rural farm life for city life.[2] In fact Nicholas Lemann argues in *The Promised Land: The Great Black Migration and How It Changed America* that what are called lower-class lifestyles are really rural lifestyles blacks brought with them when they left the rural South.[3] I discuss culture and class in more detail in Chapter 3. To continue the analysis of race thinking by blacks, take the case of the black college student who thinks racism explains why he or she receives poor grades. I worked with many black students when I taught at Rutgers

University, and I found many to have a severe lack of confidence in themselves. Too many of my black students believed they were less intelligent than their white counterparts and consequently did not put forth the kind of effort that was needed. I understood this problem and tried to instill that sense of confidence, because I was once a black college student and I too had suffered these same feelings. I would dare say a number of African Americans in all walks of life share similar feelings of inadequacy. But rather than confront the feeling itself (which, after, all is a common feeling among all peoples), too many blacks chalk it up to "racism."

African Americans can correctly blame white racism for helping create these feelings of inadequacy, but not for the continuation of these feelings. Continuing to feel inadequate, continuing to feel inferior is self-perpetuating. How I feel about myself depends not on what white people may think of me, but on what I think of myself. Feelings of low self-esteem and inferiority appear to be part of a larger problem in America. Many white people suffer from these feelings. In fact, the entire self-help phenomenon today is predicated on helping people overcome their low self-esteem and feelings of inadequacy (which create a number of addictions, aberrations in behavior, and dysfunctional families). For many blacks, these normal feelings (in today's society) get intermingled with race. Instead of dealing with low self-esteem and feelings of inadequacy as part of the human condition in twentieth-century America, African Americans allow them to take on a more ominous social, political, and racial significance. The benefit African Americans obtain from holding racism to blame for most of life's problems is a moral superiority over white people.

The price African Americans pay for holding onto this

vision of racism is a heavy one. As Glenn Loury, a black professor at Harvard, points out, even successful African Americans are not really happy: "The vicissitudes of life, the slights, the failure to get a job or a rude word from a supervisor, all are due to race."[4] Loury goes on to talk about African Americans having a mild form of paranoia, which goes hand in hand with believing oneself to be a victim. If the evils of racism have done one thing, it is to create this cult of victims.

What is the moral benefit of being a victim? Joseph Epstein wrote in a 1989 *New York Times Magazine* article that some segments of our society are becoming professional victims: "One senses that victims enjoy the moral vantage their victimhood gives them to overstate their case, to absolve themselves from all responsibility, to ask for the impossible and then to show outrage when it isn't delivered."[5] Also, and most important, victims are not responsible for their plight or actions. If you ask a victim, "Why do you smoke crack?" he will answer in terms of victimization, for example, society, being poor, or having no job. Victims rarely take responsibility for their own actions. Yet only when they do take responsibility will they stop being victims and take control of their lives. It is a healthy sign that there is a debate about victimization currently going on among blacks. New voices, such as those of William Raspberry and Shelby Steele, say it is time to drop or mute the victim claims against whites and stress individual effort and the values needed to get ahead. The tragedy of black power in America, writes Steele, is that "it is primarily a victim's power. . . . Whatever gains this power brings in the short run through political action, it undermines in the long run. Social victims may be collectively entitled, but they are all too often individually demoralized."[6]

But what fuels the notion that blacks should stress their victim role? Is it black politics or the strategic idea, by black leadership, that there is power in grievance politics? And why shouldn't these leaders believe in this approach? After all, grievance politics or the redress of grievances was what brought about the successes of the civil rights movement. In the 1960s, during the movement, America underwent a radical change. Rather than being entitled to rights as individual citizens, people were entitled collectively—blacks, women, Hispanics—in the name of redressing their grievances. According to Steele and others, this has led to separate facilities on campuses, separate study programs, and affirmative action policies. Today there is an entrenched view that group entitlement, not individual effort, is the most appropriate vehicle of black advancement.

Once grievance politics, particularly under the leadership of Martin Luther King, Jr., held the moral high ground, but today it has degenerated into racial polarization, and the victim stance has mutated into an array of conspiracy theories. One example of such a theory is the notion that some black officials are going to jail not just because they are crooked, but because of racist prosecutions, says Benjamin Hooks of the NAACP. Another theory asks: Why are one-quarter of young black males behind bars, on probation, or dead by age thirty? Hooks answers his own question: "It's not the high rate of black crime and black-on-black homicide but because whites have made black males a hunted and endangered species."[7] Vivian Gordon, a black-studies professor, asks a similar rhetorical question: Why are drugs so prevalent in the ghetto? Because whites are using substance abuse as "an instrument of genocide."[8] None of these theories speaks in the least about the responsibility of those who are in jail or using drugs. But other conspiracy theories do manage to blame the alleged hostility of Jews and the success of Korean grocers as reasons for black degradation in the ghetto. One black writer seriously argued recently that the naming of the fourth black Miss America was an attempt to keep black males down by raising up black females.[9] Unfortunately these arguments are coming not from the margins of the black community, but mainly from activists and academics, which could be a bad omen for the future. As Shelby Steele has argued, the permanent role of the victim is a trap, particularly as it is passed on to black children. It can function as a blanket excuse to explain any negative outcome as an excuse not to try. The rhetoric of victimization reinforces the view that the poor and the demoralized are little more than observers of their own lives. It teaches the young that they cannot be expected to succeed, except perhaps as part of a complaining victim group. It mocks the connection between striving and success. It makes black–white alliances unlikely, and it subtly depicts black success as a kind of commodity that whites control and refuse to dole out to the masses of blacks.

BLACK ANGER AND
THE RHETORIC OF VICTIMIZATION

A recent book by Ellis Cose, *The Rage of a Privileged Class*, asks the question: "Why are middle-class blacks angry?" Cose, a black journalist and former page editor of the *New York Daily News*, goes on to answer the somewhat rhetorical question through a series of interviews with middle-class blacks. He finds that most blacks in the middle class are filled with rage. Says Cose, "Again and again as I spoke with people who had every accouterment of success, I

heard the same plaintive declaration. . . . 'I have done everything I was supposed to do. I have stayed out of trouble with
the law, gone to the right schools. . . . Why in God's name
won't they accept me as a full human being?' "[10] Yet Cose
says later in his book, "I am not saying or suggesting that
most whites are 'racist.' The majority emphatically are not—
at least not in any meaningful sense of the word. If a racist is
defined as one who hates blacks (or members of any other
racial group, for that matter), the number of true racists is
very small."[11]

Cose's book, which is well researched and thought out,
is in the grand tradition of most current black intellectual
thinking. But he also hints at an answer to why blacks are so
angry when he says he hopes his interviews with this highly
successful group will "put that anger in the context of the
hopes, fears, and insecurities that come with being human,
irrespective of race."[12] I do not mean to discount Cose's
view—or the views of many others—that race does matter.
My view is that most blacks have become so obsessed with
race and have such sensitivity to it that they do "exhibit a
mild form of paranoia," as Glenn Loury, the black Harvard
sociologist, stated. I also believe that black anger, by both
the middle and the underclass, is not only expected but
encouraged by the larger white liberal academic and political establishment. For example, take the 1992 Los Angeles
riots and the white liberal reactions to it. Most of the liberal
intellectual response to the riots emphasized the need to
"understand the rage" of the rioters.

For most reporters, academics, politicians, and the civil
rights establishment, blacks who burned and rioted were
not criminals, but people enraged by injustice. One prominent black liberal, Representative John Conyers, Jr., a Democrat from Michigan, announced, "Those weren't criminals,

those were outraged citizens."[13] One has to wonder if there is any crime a black could have committed during the riots that Congressman Conyers would have condemned as criminal. Senator Bill Bradley of New Jersey, often identified as a moderate liberal, described the riots as "desperation and anger that boiled over into sickening violence."[14] And for five consecutive days after the riots ended, the *Los Angeles Times* published special supplements on "the roots of the riots." One day, the entire supplement was entitled "Witness to Rage." The cover of an issue of *U.S. News & World Report* featured only two words: "Race and Rage." Professor Andrew Hacker, a chief liberal spokesman on race, lends legitimacy to black rage in *Two Nations Black and White: Separate, Hostile and Equal*. Right after the riots, the *Los Angeles Times* published long excerpts from his book on its opinion page. Hacker stated, "At times, the conclusion seems all but self-evident that white America has no desire for your presence or any need for your people. Can this nation have an unstated strategy for annihilating your people? How else, you ask yourself, can one explain the incidence of death and debilitation from drugs and disease; the incarceration of a whole generation of your men; the consignment of millions of women and children to half-lives of poverty and dependence? . . . Just as your people were once made to serve silently as slaves, could it be that if white America begins to conclude that you are becoming too much trouble, it will find itself contemplating more lasting solutions?"[15] When the leading white liberal "expert" on race relations in America tells blacks that America wishes to exterminate them and the newspaper of the city in which the riots occurred publishes this a week after the riots, one can understand the legitimizing of black rage.

Less than a week after the riots the *Los Angeles Times* published on its opinion page the following statement of black liberal author Walter Mosely: "America is a brutal land. Its language is violence and bloodshed. That is why [Rodney] King was beaten; that is why another King was assassinated."[16] On the same opinion page, the same day, the *Times* published a piece by Leon Litwack, Morrison Professor of American History at the University of California at Berkeley. He says, "The lawlessness began with the clubbing of black America, the conscious and criminal neglect and fashionable racism characteristic of the Age of Greed, over which Ronald Reagan and George Bush have presided."[17] Leonard Fein, another prominent liberal writer, stated after the riots, "We have, as a nation, decided to bequeath to our children the rotten fruit of racism and bigotry, decided that it will be for them to choke on it. . . . We must stop now the persistent looting of human life, end the stealing of hope and the torching of health."[18] Adding fuel to the fires was another angry black liberal spokesman, the Reverend James Lawson of Los Angeles, who said after the riot, "The rioters and looters were doing exactly what the United States had done to the men, women and children of Central American countries and in the Persian Gulf War."[19]

Given the above statements by both white and black liberal scholars, it is a wonder that all blacks in Los Angeles did not riot. But the liberal intellectual community has been preaching this sermon for years. And in the face of this litany, how could any self-respecting black person not be angry? Yet as Glenn Loury stated, this anger also leads to unhappiness and a "mild form of paranoia." Middle-class blacks are overwhelmingly college graduates, and on college campuses they are taught that America is racist. A few years ago, Harvard sponsored a week-long program against racism called AWARE ("Actively Working against Racism and Ethnocentrism"), at which students learned from the keynote speaker, Professor John Dovidio of Colgate, that 85 percent of white Americans harbor some form of racism and the other 15 percent are outright racists.[20] They also heard a Dartmouth dean say that major American universities are "genocidal in nature." And the president of Occidental College in Los Angeles said not long ago that blacks on predominantly white campuses "face a level of hatred, prejudice and ignorance comparable to that of the days of Bull Connor, Lester Maddox and Orval Faubus."[21]

I can remember being on college campuses during the 1960s, 1970s, and 1980s and don't remember this virulent level of racism. In fact, what I do remember is a number of white liberal professors and students being, if anything, overly solicitous toward black students.[22] It is from academia, after all, that we get the strongest affirmative action programs. The complaint by many of my black colleagues during the 1960s and 1970s was about being patronized by whites who were overly sympathetic about our supposed ghetto sufferings. They (whites) expected us (blacks) to be angry at them and, as Shelby Steele described in *The Content of Our Character*, blacks could easily put them down using collective guilt.[23] I think it is these former college students who have become politicians, professors, and members of the American media who say to rioters and arsonists, "We understand your rage." That was certainly the message black U.S. Representative Maxine Waters wanted the rioters to hear when she screamed at a Washington, D.C., rally following the riots, "No justice, no peace." Indeed, as a reward for her fiery speech, ABC News named Maxine Waters its "Person of the Week."[24] The media, in particular, are patronizing and reluctant to criticize blacks. One incident during the riot shows just how ludicrous this reluctance can be. In an article entitled "Blacks and Liberals: The Los Angeles Riots," Dennis Prager describes a local Los Angeles reporter saying, "I see five black gentlemen throwing stones at cars."[25] According to Prager, "Liberalism has so stifled moral honesty in relation to blacks that a reporter instinctively felt it necessary to call black thugs 'gentlemen.'"[26]

THE ROOTS OF BLACK ANGER

The black middle class is discussed in detail in Chapter 3, but what of underclass black anger? Jesse Peterson is the founder of the Brotherhood Organization of a New Destiny (BOND), a Los Angeles–based group dedicated to helping black males deal with their anger at their absent fathers and often-angry mothers. Peterson is making people aware of something that should have been all too obvious: Blacks males who were abandoned by their fathers are likely to be angry males. Says Peterson, "When 60 to 70 percent of black boys grow up without fathers to be their moral models and disciplinarians, rage and violence are not surprising."[27]

Damian ("Football") Williams, the young black man accused of hitting the white truck driver Reginald Denny in the head with a brick during the Los Angeles riots, told police shortly after being arrested, "I never seen my daddy. I bet if I had a father, I wouldn't be in this predicament that I'm in right now." According to the *Los Angeles Times*, Williams said this "with his voice cracking with sobs."[28] But instead of focusing on the absence of black men to serve as fathers and civilizing role models, white and black liberals have focused on white racism. If blacks of both the middle class and the underclass are angry, so are whites. Anger, it appears, is a condition of modern-day America. Everybody from radical animal rights groups to the Gray Panthers (an organization of the elderly) are angry about their plight or cause.

Dennis Prager argues, in an earlier-cited article, that liberal whites promote black anger because they are so angry. Why are liberal whites angry? Because, says Prager, "a distinguishing feature of leftist ideology has been that it holds external factors responsible for people's spiritual, psychological and emotional angst, and for their alienation—a condition acutely felt by people on the Left. Hence, the constant tampering with government, the religious belief in the efficacy of "social policy": since the disease is social, the cure must be social policy.[29] Whether one agrees with Prager about liberalism, it is true that we all experience pain, alienation, and isolation from our fellow human beings.

As Michael Lerner, editor of the liberal magazine *Tikkun*, has written, "The breakdown of families, the crisis of friendships, the deep trouble people have in finding and sustaining long-term, committed, loving relationships—all the core issues of crisis of contemporary life—are part of the human condition."[30] But I feel that what distinguishes black anger from white anger is race and the justification race gives to us to be angry. Anger becomes not part of the human condition that we all experience, but only of the black condition that we (blacks) experience. Not all anger is bad. It was black anger that kept Rosa Parks from getting up and giving her seat to a white bus passenger in Birmingham, Alabama, in 1955. This individual anger launched the famous bus boycott and ultimately the civil rights movement.

But today's black anger tends not to be useful. It is instead the alienation that Ellis Cose describes in his book about middle-class anger. Some of his respondents' anger was so great as to cause them to "give up hope." When anger gives way to dysfunction, I think it has become tied to issues of self-esteem and self-worth. Some of Cose's middle-class respondents were unhappy because they did not feel accepted by "white society," and yet they were tremendously successful in that "society." While some of Cose's respondents did believe their careers had been held back because of race, most of his respondents were blacks who had it all—career, money, and creature comforts—yet were still angry. Why? Perhaps one reason was their looking outside themselves for validation of self. Also, acceptance is a feeling which is nebulous and hard to define. How would a black person know when the white world accepted him or her? What measure would he or she use to determine acceptance?

I think Cose hit on a deeper issue that has little to do with white racism. I don't believe we African Americans, no matter what our station in life, fully accept ourselves. The rage comes because we are still looking for white validation, which will never come. Why won't it come? Because white people don't have the power to validate blacks—any more than blacks have the power to validate whites. Validation—acceptance—comes from inside, and until we blacks understand that, we will always feel not quite part of American society. That is why other groups like Asians, Cubans, and, even to some extent, West Indian (origin) blacks can come to America and succeed when American (origin) blacks cannot. They didn't start out being told they were inferior and unacceptable. Immigrants come to America as free people looking for opportunities, not as slaves. There is no reason

for Asians who come to this country to believe themselves to
be inferior. The early Chinese immigrants who helped build
the railroads during the nineteenth century were not treated
well by white Americans, but these Chinese brought centu-
ries of culture with them which validated their self-worth.
As the highly acclaimed black economist Thomas Sowell
stated in *Civil Rights: Rhetoric or Reality?* West Indian blacks
"living in the United States are a group physically indis-
tinguishable from black Americans, but with a cultural
background that is quite different. If . . . racial discrimination is the primary determinant of below-average black income, West Indian incomes would be similarly affected. Yet
West Indian family incomes are 94 percent of the U.S. national average [based on the 1970 census], while the family
incomes of blacks as a group are only 62 percent of the
national average. West Indian 'representation' in professional occupations is double that of blacks and slightly
higher than that of the U.S. population as a whole."[31]

West Indian blacks suffered slavery during the nineteenth century, but with one important difference: They
were in a majority, and whites were in the minority. Colonial
government was said not to be as harsh as slave society.
West Indians grew up seeing others of their kind as police
officers, professionals, and so on. In America blacks enjoyed
none of this freedom until many years later and continued
to live as a minority within a majority culture. The legacy of
slavery and its aftermath did not hang as heavily around the
necks of the West Indians. West Indian blacks don't need
validation from whites to feel competent; they already know
they can run an entire country without white help or approval.

American black rage is inextricably tied to the issue of
low black self-esteem, which has been most eloquently dis-

cussed by Shelby Steele in *The Content of Our Character*. Steele says that the best way African Americans can begin to repair their feelings of low self-esteem is by developing a strong sense of individualism and an individual sense of self-worth. I tend to agree with Steele on this point, as well as with William Raspberry, a black *Washington Post* columnist, who says, "African Americans are not yet at the point where we can react in political and social terms entirely as individuals. White people can pretty much react as individuals. If whites are not doing as well as they hoped . . . they can chalk it up to either bad luck or some personal failing, whereas blacks are much more likely to conclude that . . . a major part of . . . not doing well relates to the color of our skin. And we don't dare become comfortable with our own situation as long as skin color still plays a major role in the prospects of people who look like us."[32]

That is why the belief that racism causes all our problems is primary in the African-American psyche. Black America must believe that racism is even more invidious and pernicious than ever before. If it isn't, then why aren't black people doing better? If it isn't because of racism, then how does one explain that one in four black youths between eighteen and twenty-nine are in state or local prison and that blacks commit 45 percent of violent crimes in America (1991 FBI crime statistics).[33] The black psyche is reluctant to allow racism, as the cause of all its problems, to diminish in America. Racism is an easy answer which does not require much introspection. Without racism, other issues must be explored, and some of these issues have to do with what Glenn Loury calls "moral character." African Americans have traditionally rejected discussions regarding black morality and particularly the morality of the lower classes. So we (blacks) scramble to find reasons for the unkind statistics which show a disproportionate number of our people on welfare, in jails, and having babies out of wedlock, and we quietly worry about why things have not improved more quickly for our people. The belief that racism is a sufficient explanation for the condition of many blacks in America relieves self-doubt and fear that something inherently negative about being black may be the real cause of our problems. To the extent actual racism becomes harder to use as an explanation, black voices become even more shrill in screaming racism.

Actual unambiguous racists like ex-Klan member David Duke become almost a relief because finally we can see a real one. After listening to Duke (who denies he's racist any longer), one will hear many African Americans give a satisfied sigh and say, "Well, at least he's honest." Jesse Jackson interviewed David Duke on his cable television program and treated him the way one would treat a worthy adversary. Last, real racism is not dead in America. It will probably always be with us. However, racism is not black America's worst enemy. Our worst enemy is the excuse racism provides many of us not to be the best we can be.

PLAYING THE RACE CARD

Using racial issues to manipulate white people became possible only after the advent of the civil rights movement. Before the civil rights movement, racial prejudice was not universally condemned. "Playing the race card" is a form of power used by blacks to gain moral authority over white people who are presumed guilty of some racial infraction. White males in particular have benefited immensely from being white and therefore are morally vulnerable to a charge of racism whether individually guilty or not. As was said earlier, U.S. Supreme Court Justice Clarence Thomas "played the race card" during his Senate confirmation hearings. He called the hearings a "hi-tech lynching reserved for uppity blacks."

Using the "race card" is similar to using the joker in a deck of cards. The joker is a "wild card" that has powers above the other cards. It can make a weak card hand strong. This analogy explains how race is used by blacks to manipulate whites. No matter what the merits of a particular position or point of view, once race is introduced the other issues are compromised.

Blacks are not the only group to use the "race card." The Jewish community uses the "anti-Semitic card," particularly in defending Israel. Whenever Israel is criticized, the critical people are suspected of having an ulterior motive, that is, anti-Semitism. In fact, it seems that everyone has a "card" to play when it comes to taking responsibility for her or his own actions. Recently Lorena Bobbitt, the woman who cut off her husband's penis, was exonerated by a jury because she played her "battered-wife" card. The famous (or infamous) brothers who murdered their parents with shotguns, Lyle and Erik Menendez, were able to convince a jury that they had been sexually abused by their father. While they were not freed, the jury was unable to convict them, and another trial will have to be conducted. Their defense for these cold-blooded killings was their "child-abuse" card.

The most repugnant example of not taking responsibility for one's actions has been suggested by Colin Ferguson's attorney, William Kunstler. Ferguson is the black man who killed six people on a Long Island Railroad train because he didn't like white people (one of the victims was an Asian woman). According to Kunstler, Mr. Ferguson's defense will be "black rage." What is the black rage defense? Says the attorney, Ferguson's life as a black man in America was so mentally stressful for him that he snapped and started killing the source of his anger: whites.

What is frightening about this defense is not that some defense attorney would use it, but the support some black leaders have given to it. Of course, this defense opens up our society to anyone's rage, from Lorena Bobbitt's to Harvey Fierstein's (he is a prominent writer and gay activist). Everyone in America who feels abused or oppressed could go out into the street and start shooting those they believe to be the perpetrators of that oppression. And in such a society, life would be, as the nineteenth-century English philosopher Thomas Hobbes stated, "solitary, poor, nasty, brutish, and short." Hobbes was speaking about a society in which there was no social contract (law).

It is not surprising that lawyers are the culprits behind many of these "I am not responsible" defenses. Lawyers, after all, are paid advocates. They play a role in our society very similar to that played by the Sophists in ancient Greece. (The Sophists were professional debaters during the time of Socrates. The Sophists debated to win arguments, not to discover truth, which is the purpose of any real debate—at least the Greeks thought so.)

Today, everyone, or so it seems, is playing a "guilt" card of one kind or another. But for blacks, playing the race card is particularly destructive because it keeps blacks in the role of victim. Clarence Thomas (today he is a U.S. Supreme Court Associate Justice) lost personal power when he played the race card. He admitted that he really was an affirmative action candidate and, in evoking race, tacitly requested that the Senate Judiciary Committee vote for him because of his race. Yet these are issues to which, supposedly, a black conservative like Clarence Thomas is opposed. When blacks play the race card, they are buying into a certain mean-spiritedness that does not empower them. It is a cynical attempt to manipulate whites through guilt. Those who play the card are acquiescing to the notion of black inferiority by admitting, as did Clarence Thomas, that race, after all, is the deciding factor.

At a news conference some years ago, former black Congressman Gus Savage (representing South Chicago) stated, "Racism is white . . . there ain't no black racism." The dictionary defines *racism* as the belief that one's own race is superior to another race. What Savage and other blacks who agree with him are saying is that racism, as practiced in America, has always been a relationship of the power of one race over another. Since blacks have no power to impose a racist agenda on whites, then blacks cannot be truly racists. The problem with this definition is that it misses several vital points. First, blacks have grown stronger over the years and are not in the same subordinate position as in years past. Second, most blacks, including Gus Savage, are believers in black power, and to say blacks can't be racists is to accept a position of powerlessness forever.

Blacks can certainly be prejudiced against others. This has been seen during the virulent anti-Asian demonstrations that have occurred in several cities over the last few years. Much of the anger expressed by blacks against Korean merchants has had racial overtones. In fact, Asians have found themselves subject to fire bombings and other racist attacks, like the three Asian boys who were beaten (one almost to death) by a group of black youths. Why were these Asians beaten? Because they were Asian. And look at the anti-Semitic language of Khalil Mohammed, the Black Muslim spokesman and follower of Farrakhan. Mohammed has become known of late for his diatribes against Jews. More about him will be discussed in a later chapter.

RACIAL OBSESSION

Not only blacks but everyone in America is obsessed with race. Race has become larger than life to many Americans and is the national pastime. For example, as of this writing, America is now consumed with the O. J. Simpson murder mystery. This is the case of a man accused of killing his wife and her friend. But already race has reared its ugly head because O. J. Simpson is black and his wife was white. Regardless of his innocence or guilt, the issue is one of passion, love, and violence—not race. Yet the media have done a series of polls asking respondents if they felt Simpson could get a fair trial and whether they (the respondents) were sympathetic to Simpson. Blacks were overwhelmingly sympathetic, and whites were not. A majority of blacks didn't think he could get a fair trial, and a majority of whites thought he could. First of all, it is not unusual for an ethnic group to feel sympathy for one of its heroes and particularly someone as popular as Simpson. I can personally say that there was a great deal of disappointment in the black community, at least in Los Angeles, over the fact that Simpson found himself in such a predicament. The mass media seem to be the ones exploiting the race issue by the polls they have taken and the discussions regarding race they have encouraged. I think it has been remarkable that the story has remained as focused on race as it has continued to be. The Simpson case points out that even when situations occur in our society which are not racial, they become racial because of America's obsession with race.

Black people must resist this obsession because it usually only reminds them that they are victims in America. The
racial fixation feeds into a feeling that all things are determined by race and are therefore outside one's control. It is
time to get outside the obsession and move toward a more
individualistic approach to events. There is nothing about
the Simpson murder case that is racial except the races of the
victims and of the accused. This case or any other is a race
issue only because blacks and whites make it so. In some
regards I think blacks are more guilty than whites of making
situations racial ones. Let's take the poll data in the Simpson
case. If he were a popular white sports hero, how sympathetic would blacks be? And more important, would the
issue of race even come up? Would the media run a poll and
analyze the data by race? I think not. In the end, black
people lose in a racially polarized environment. It is time for
racial healing, which I discuss in Chapter 9.

CHAPTER TWO

Race or Class?
A Classic Debate

As I argued earlier, racism has become a definitive concept for black America. For many it helps explain why more blacks have not been successful in America. However, by focusing on racism, black America has tended to ignore a disturbing trend: the formation of a black underclass. Until recently, liberal social scientists in general and black scholars in particular have resisted acknowledging the very existence of a black underclass. William Julius Wilson, who is credited with starting the debate over the underclass and urban policy, has begun to regret using the term *underclass*. Wilson believes it has certain negative connotations which he never intended.[1] Despite the debate over what constitutes an underclass and who are its members, most agree that such a class exists, although the controversy continues.[2] However, once the existence of a black underclass is acknowledged, its existence seriously challenges notions about racism. The concept of *class* connotes a series of values and modes of behavior that have less to do with racial group than with economic status. Marxist ideology defines *class* as one's economic status vis-à-vis the ruling order. For Marx, the lower classes were defined by their economic status in relationship to those who owned the means of production. Modern post-Marxist class definitions see class as both economic status and moral values. Class becomes a lifestyle issue. A person with lower-class values acts in certain ways which are not productive to his or her advancement. But class cuts across racial lines, which means there are other races that have lower-class members. In a strictly class analysis, poor whites would act the same as do poor blacks in terms of their behavior and lifestyle. They act similarly to poor blacks because it is class, not race, which defines them. The same is true of middle-class blacks and whites in terms of their behavior and values.

What disturbs those who use racism rather than class as the reason blacks have not progressed faster in America is that class contradicts race as the sole culprit. A class analysis brings into play other explanatory factors, such as moral values, economic forces, and lifestyles. A racial analysis uses only one factor, race or racism, as an explanation for lack of black progress. When Wilson wrote *The Declining Significance of Race*, he tried to show that race could no longer be used to explain the pathologies of black life. He argued that class differences explain much more about black ills than does race because of successes brought about by the civil rights movement during the 1960s. Wilson also challenges those who argue that the urban poor are simply a result of a "racist" society. He states, "I think there is no way you can understand the current situation, the disproportionate number of blacks in the underclass, without considering the historic effects of racism. But the sharp increases in the rates of social dislocation since 1970—that is, joblessness, the increase in female-headed families, welfare dependency, and related problems—cannot be placed at the feet of racism. Racism created the large black underclass and then stepped aside and watched changes in the economy cement blacks into that underclass. And the problem is that many liberal advocates of anti-poverty and anti-discrimination programs often tried to explain the increasing rates of social dislocation in terms of racism, but this just didn't wash."[3]

Implicit in Wilson's argument, however, is the notion that culture is defined by structural forces and not the reverse. Social stratification in terms of class is determined by economic structure, which in turn is influenced by world economic changes. The black underclass, according to Wilson, came about because of a changing availability of jobs for inner-city dwellers.

Where once a sociologist like Oliver Cox, who wrote a landmark book in 1949 called *Caste, Class and Race*, could discuss race as the most important factor in understanding black life in America, he would no longer be able to do so today, according to Professor Wilson. Class analysis is not new in American social science research. But in recent years, mainly conservative social scientists, like Charles Murray, who wrote *Losing Ground*, have used this approach to discuss the black condition in America.[4] Conservative social scientists like Murray have used class arguments to make policy recommendations to the federal government. They argue that welfare spending on blacks helped create black dependency and consequently a ghetto underclass.[5] For the most part, the conservatives have been reluctant to say that racism had any causative relationship in the formation of this ghetto lower class.[6] On the other side are black scholars and liberal social scientists who have denied, until quite recently, that a black underclass even exists.[7]

Even when a liberal white social scientist like Daniel Patrick Moynihan, then Assistant Secretary of Labor, tried to address the possibility that an underclass was developing, he endured fierce criticism. In 1964 he issued a policy paper, "The Negro Family: The Case for National Action." Now known as the Moynihan Report, the paper argued that if black poverty was to be eradicated, blacks would have to gain not only the same opportunities as whites but also the same resources for taking advantage of these opportunities. Yet, the report went on, the breakdown of the black family through divorce, separation, and desertion was depriving black children of at least two prime determinants of achievement: discipline and emotional support. "The present tangle of pathology," wrote Moynihan, "is capable of perpetuating itself without assistance from the white world. Programs to wipe out black poverty will fail unless they are designed to have the effect, directly or indirectly, of enhancing the stability and resources of the Negro American family."[8] At the time of Moynihan's writing, the female-headed family was already a salient feature of the black community. Accordingly, the initial reaction of many black leaders was favorable. Other black leaders felt, however, that calling for changes in black behavior would slacken the nation's commitment to racial equality. They responded angrily, branding Moynihan a "subtle racist."[9]

As the controversy heated up, most of the black leaders who had endorsed the report's thesis repositioned themselves, as did "progressive" white politicians, journalists, clerics, and academics, most for fear of being tainted with the charge of racism. A few social scientists noted that Moynihan's paper deserved serious, dispassionate study, but their voices were drowned out by loud protests. "There was a massive failure of nerve among whites," observed Moynihan in a retrospective account, "a spare number of academics excepted."[10] The Moynihan Report was thus brushed aside, even as the problems it identified deepened.

Two decades would pass before its thesis was reintroduced into academic discourse, and three decades later, few researchers are seeking to build on its insights.

Today, because of Moynihan's pioneering work on the decline of the black family and Wilson's work on the black underclass, most black and white liberal social scientists are willing to accept the term *black underclass*, though reluctantly. However, unlike conservatives, they argue that this underclass was created by too little social spending, not too much.[11] Why are discussions of the culture of poverty and the ghetto underclass so frightening to black scholars and liberal social scientists? One reason is the undermining of racism as one of the main causative factors in the continuation of the black underclass. These scholars are afraid, according to Wilson, that if racism's role in sustaining the underclass is reduced, the conservative argument will prevail.

This is an unfounded fear because clearly, as Wilson points out in an earlier quote, historical racism did contribute to the formation of a black underclass. Racism restricted the opportunities for blacks to enter mainstream America. What is argued, by Wilson and others, is that the continuation of lower-class lifestyles can no longer be explained simply in terms of race.[12] As I previously stated, once race is removed, other more frightening possibilities come to light. Questions about morality and dysfunctional behavior are raised by scholars like Glenn Loury and Thomas Sowell. Both Loury and Sowell are distinguished black scholars who argue that it is a lack of moral character which accounts for why so many blacks are members of this underclass.

Is there something about the very nature of Americans of African descent that facilitates a ghetto culture? Is this ghetto culture really a sharecropper culture that blacks

brought north in the great migration which Nicholas Lemann writes about in *The Promised Land: The Great Black
Migration*? Lemann's argument is that today's ghetto culture
is really a continuation of a sharecropper culture blacks had
when living in the rural South. To understand what kind of
culture 5 million blacks brought north after 1940 (a migration larger than that of the Italians or Jews), Lemann went
south to Clarksdale, Mississippi, which was a point of de-
parture for the families he followed. Lemann describes a
sharecropper culture that is rife with drunkenness, illegitimacy, and other problems fueled by the racism of white
planters, who usually cheated their black tenants. Black
tenants in turn tried to cheat the whites by picking cotton in
a slipshod manner that allowed them to earn more when
their harvests were weighed. According to Lemann, blacks
learned early to hustle the whites for survival, and he fol-
lows this ethic north where, he argues, it got worse. Lemann
makes his culture-of-poverty argument by following Ruby
Haynes, a black sharecropper, and her family in their twenty-
two-year struggle in Chicago.

For Ruby Haynes, Mississippi (to which she would
eventually return) and Chicago were equally ridden with
crime, poverty, and bad men. Lemann paints a rather sad
picture of ghetto life, and what is worse, he implies it is inevitable because of a kind of cultural determinism. Lemann
denies he holds such a fatalistic vision and has a number of
liberal prescriptions for turning ghetto life around. But
culture-of-poverty issues are even more frightening to
blacks than the specter of racism because they raise questions about the very nature of the black experience in America. Could the black experience have created a cultural determinism that has continued to today? If so, how can a

person's culture be changed? These are not questions easily answered.

Loury has argued that even if all racism disappeared tomorrow, some blacks would still live a lower-class existence. Wilson agrees with him and states, "There are some blacks for whom it is enough to remove the artificial barriers of race. After that, their entry into the American mainstream is virtually automatic; there are others for whom hardly anything would change, if by some magical stroke, racism disappeared from America. Everyone knows this of course. And hardly anyone is willing to say it. And because we don't say it, we wind up confused about how to deal with the explosive problems confronting the American society, confused about what the problem really is."[13] Four hundred years of oppression in America have caused many of us (blacks) to be vulnerable to self-doubt. In our deepest subconscious mind we wonder if we can make it in America even if the playing field is equal. It is within the context of this uncertainty and confusion that black scholars have resisted a thorough analysis that might explain the formation of a black underclass.

BLACK CLASS DIVISIONS

Historically the black middle class has been a very beleaguered and maligned group. While many blacks belong to it, there appears to be some resistance to being called middle class. It is not surprising. The black middle class has been excoriated by no less a historical giant than E. Franklin Frazier. Frazier was the first black chairman of the sociology department at Howard University. In his 1957 book *The Black*

Bourgeoisie, he traced the black middle class from slavery days to the then-present. According to Franklin, there was a division among black slaves into field and house Negroes. While the field Negroes were a hard-working, noble group, the house Negroes were an untrustworthy lot. Pampered by their white masters, they thought themselves better than field Negroes. They also strongly identified with the white master, taking on his airs. Malcolm X, in the documentary *By Any Means Necessary*, parodied the house slaves. He said that when the white master was sick, the house slave would say, "What's the matter, master, are *we* sick?" House Negroes were accused of informing on field Negroes and thwarting slave uprisings and escape plots. According to Franklin, from these house Negroes originated the black middle class.

That portrait of house versus field slaves remains a part of black folklore today and makes it understandable why many blacks are not comfortable with the term *middle class*. Feeling guilty about their status, many middle-class blacks try to identify with lower-class blacks and in so doing make these (poor) blacks the standard for all blacks. Yet the black middle-class lifestyle is the opposite of the lower-class lifestyle. It is largely made up of two-parent households, and while income still lags behind that of white households, it is well above the poverty line. As was stated in the Introduction, the proportion of black households earning $50,000 or more a year rose from 5.3 to 12.1 percent, while the proportion earning $100,000 and up in those same years more than doubled, from 0.5 percent to 1.2 percent. One would think that black America would be proud of its middle class, but it is not. In *Faces at the Bottom of the Well*, Derrick Bell, a black civil rights activist and legal scholar, puts into the mouth of a black cab driver addressing a black professional a strong

indictment of the black middle class: "I mean you no of-
fense," says the driver, "but the fact is you movin'-on-up
black folks hurt us everyday blacks simply by being successful. The white folks see you doing your thing, making
money in the high five figures, latching onto all kinds of
fancy titles, some of which even have a little authority behind the name and generally moving on up. They conclude
right off that discrimination is over, and that if the rest of
us got off our dead asses, dropped the welfare tit, stopped
having illegitimate babies, and found jobs, we would all be
just like you."[14]

It appears that Bell's mythical cab driver resents the
success of the black middle class, but in reality the cab driver
represents black middle-class guilt. It is not unusual for the
black middle class to be frequently attacked by members of
its own group. Alvin Poussaint, famous black Harvard psy-
chiatrist, has written, "Some successful (black) men and
women claim to feel no obligation to less fortunate blacks
and are angry and resentful when it is suggested that they
owe something to others."[15] Poussaint goes on to say that
these same blacks turn white rejection into bitterness toward other blacks instead of toward white racists. He then
says, "Some blacks (middle-class) who believe they are paying the price for the antisocial and unacceptable actions of
'low-class' blacks may express pro-racist attitudes, ratio-
nalizing them as objective judgments. Asking such affluent
blacks to aid black community causes often evokes anger
and responses like, 'I made it on my own. Why can't they?' "
Poussaint's beliefs about the black middle class are not
unique or unusual. He and many other members of the
black middle class have disdain for members of their own
group, because surely Dr. Poussaint is a middle-class black.
Why this disdain, and where does it come from? Much of

Dr. Poussaint's discussion is entirely anecdotal. He offers no empirical proof of his statements about black middle-class attitudes. But he is not alone in his negative views. Nathan Hare, a prominent black writer and intellectual, says, "But they (middle-class blacks) are resented for their bourgeois airs, White mimicry, social dalliance and courting of opulence and extravagance. At the same time they are unable to gain unqualified access to the white race whose ideals and standards and (occasionally) physiognomy they openly and unashamedly adopt as their own."[16]

The disdain that middle-class blacks have for other middle-class blacks is driven home by the following example. As in Chapter 1, we visit the famous case of ex-football star and celebrity O. J. Simpson. At the time this is being written, Simpson is awaiting trial for murdering his ex-wife and her friend. Simpson, a beloved national football hero for both white and black people, is not thought of so highly by some middle-class blacks. Here is what some of these blacks thought of Simpson taken from a piece written by Ellis Cose, a previously cited writer and former reporter, for *Newsweek* (July 11, 1994). Says Cose, "He [Simpson] was widely seen as an affable nonmenacing paragon of black manhood and a reassuring example of an African-American accepted in the mainstream world. . . . Now Simpson's efforts to minimize race are widely mocked. *Sports Illustrated* portrays him as a man who made himself so self effacing and eager to please that he was deemed nonthreatening to whites. . . . Playthell Benjamin, a columnist for the *New York Daily News*, dismisses him as "what the old folks used to call a 'white folks' Negro.' " Cose goes on to quote an old country club friend of Simpson's as saying, "See, O.J. thought he was white. He acted white. . . . He married a white woman."[17]

Notice that the people Cose quoted, including himself, were all middle-class blacks. How would they have Simpson or any celebrity act? Like a gang member? What is acting white? Smiling and speaking correct English? Should a black person act ignorant or uneducated to be black? Cose also seems to take particular exception to Simpson's playing golf. He states, "His efforts to minimize race are being mocked—he even played golf."[18] What's wrong with playing golf? Should black men play only basketball? Cose tries to say that Simpson's attempts to blend into the larger society (white world) alienated some of his support in the black community, but he then contradicts himself by citing a *Los Angeles Times* poll which showed that 74 percent of blacks were very or somewhat sympathetic to Simpson, compared to only 34 percent of whites. I also suspect that most of the criticism of Simpson comes from middle-class blacks like those cited in Cose's article and not from the black masses, who continue to be the bedrock of his support.

Yet despite these attacks, most blacks strive to be middle class, they want better jobs, comfortable homes, and nice cars to drive. In a word, they want the American dream. To obtain these things, middle-class blacks started the entire civil rights movement of the 1950s and 1960s. The famous lunch-counter sit-ins were headed by black college students throughout the South. They were joined by white college students and formed the Student Non-Violent Coordinating Committee (SNCC). Black middle-class leadership was responsible for the passage of the 1965 Voting Rights Act, which enabled southern blacks to vote in large numbers. Because of black voting, the number of black elected officials has increased from less than 200 during the 1950s to over 6,500 today.[19]

Much can be said for the political and social activism of the black middle class. Yet, paradoxically, there is a great deal of self-doubt and self-loathing in members of this same group. Could the black middle class be suffering from a collective psychological phenomenon called *survivor's guilt*, similar to that of Jews who escaped the concentration camps or American soldiers who came back from Vietnam without a scratch? Just like the Jews who escaped the Holocaust, many middle-class blacks have escaped a similar death in the ghetto—if not physical death, then a death of the spirit. Black middle-class guilt explains why this group is so anxious to provide an alibi and rationale for the behavior of lower-class blacks. For example, during the 1992 Los Angeles riots, I heard several of my black friends try to justify the riot, calling it a rebellion. I would ask them why they weren't out on the street participating. The answer was quite obvious: They weren't out there because they had too much to lose, such as mortgages, jobs, and cars. I also pointed out that, historically, most rebellions were directed against the establishment, which in many cases my friends represented.

A case in point was the burning of the Aquarius Book Store, the only black-owned bookstore in Los Angeles. This bookstore had been in Los Angeles for years. It championed African American culture in the books it stocked. After the bookstore was burned, its owner, who had previously considered himself a champion of black causes, was interviewed. He was at a loss to explain the reason. It was a deliberate act, and the owner said those who had burned him out "did not come in here to read about Malcolm X." There were more examples of blacks' being burned out during the riots through deliberate acts. Why did this happen? Because many rioters wanted to burn out store owners whom they perceived to be members of the establishment. Unfortunately this definition included several middle-class blacks, such as the owner of the bookstore.

But when the rioting ended and while the fires were still smoldering, one could hear middle-class black leaders busily trying to justify to the media the burning down of the city. Privately, I believe, these acts of burning and looting embarrassed and chagrined the black middle class. They offended the middle-class sense of what proper behavior ought to be. But publicly, these blacks trudged forward to defend actions which they themselves would not take to voice a grievance. Middle-class blacks and whites did what the middle class does to protest: They held meetings and prayer vigils. Local black politicians and neighborhood leaders suggested that they organize protest rallies to register disapproval of the Rodney King verdict, which sparked the unrest.[20] Those who burned the city were not members of this group. They acted because they had nothing to lose. Two-thirds of those arrested were Hispanics, many newly arrived from places like El Salvador and Honduras. The majority had probably never heard of Rodney King.

Part of the blame for the riot has to be placed on the black middle class. When they moved out of Los Angeles, they removed a very strong stabilizing force. They were home owners and promoted neighborhood cohesiveness. For the most part, their kids stayed in school, their daughters didn't get pregnant, and their sons didn't go to jail. The middle class provided a bridge to the larger society's values. But once they left, those role models were no longer there. This is true when the black middle class moves out of all inner-city areas.

It is difficult to tell people they can be successful when there are no concrete examples of success that they can observe. Ghetto underclass lifestyles, as Professor Wilson describes them in his book, are not mainstream. These lifestyles perpetuate negative social behaviors like crime, drug usage, welfare dependency, and family instability. What is even more disturbing is the growth of this ghetto underclass over the last fifteen to twenty years. Its growth is like a cancer. In virtually every economic category, life in the ghetto is worse today than twenty years ago. The growth of this group of blacks poses a threat to America of untold proportions. While racism and discrimination add to the problems of a ghetto underclass, they do not explain its growth. Never before have so many poor blacks lived so close together in such poverty. (Professor Wilson calls this the "concentration effect.") Black urban poverty, which appears to be different from rural poverty, has created social conditions that are wildly at odds with the promise of a humane and secure social order.

THE STRUCTURALLY UNEMPLOYED

Professor Wilson, in a series of books and articles, has argued that while the problems facing blacks in earlier periods of American history could be primarily attributed to racism, recent economic changes have put a greater weight on class than on race. In particular, urban blacks, who entered the labor market in large numbers during the boom years of the 1960s, have begun to lose jobs because jobs have left them. We face a serious structural mismatch, says Wilson, because jobs exist in the suburbs, or even abroad, while unskilled workers live in the city. The costs of bringing the two together are high, and urban blacks pay those costs. Over the last twenty years, America's economic base has changed from a goods-producing to an information-processing economy. Consequently, workers who in the past were able to obtain relatively high-paying jobs which required low education can no longer do so. Also, recent studies have shown that whereas a high school diploma or less was sufficient to work in many industries in 1970, it became more necessary to have some college by 1984.[21] That trend has become even more evident today.

My father, with only a fourth-grade education, was able to earn a decent middle-class living during the 1950s, 1960s, and 1970s. He drove a truck and later became a tool crib operator for an aerospace company. What would my father's potential for earning a good middle-class income be in 1994? Not very good. At the same time workers needed more education to obtain good-paying jobs, blacks were dropping out of high school in higher numbers.[22] A question we need to ask in the black community is why these kids leave. Is it because schools are worse today than years ago? Are the children worse? Are they less respectful of teachers and authority?

I went to an all-black high school in South Central Los Angeles during the early 1960s. There were street gangs in existence, but not even the worst gang member would have thought of attacking a teacher. Gang fights consisted of a few bloody noses or split lips, and when compared to today's carnage, those earlier fights seem mild. Can racism be blamed for making today's black youth less respectful of teachers than we were years ago? Can racism explain what appears to be the complete disregard for human life which some gang members exhibit when they do drive-by shootings? I would argue that schools were more institutionally racist in 1960 than they are today. During my school days, black children were routinely "tracked" into low-level occupations by standardized tests. Depending on how you scored, you could be placed in either a college-preparatory curriculum or a lower-level course of study. The black kids tended to end up in classes for the academically slow. I can remember a white high school counselor telling me, based on my test scores, that I should look into becoming a cook rather than the lawyer I said I wanted to be. I went home and told my parents, who said that the counselor was wrong, possibly a racist, and that I should disregard what she had said. I had teachers who were openly contemptuous of black students and who were only in our high school because they could go nowhere else.

Clearly things were worse then and are better today. But even if ghetto schools are as racist today as they were years ago, that does not explain why conditions in ghetto schools are so much worse today. The level of violence is much higher today than in 1960. We had no drive-by shootings in those days. Our idea of drugs in school was someone smoking cigarettes in the boys' bathroom. Why are ghetto schools worse today? One explanation is that ghetto parents are not in as much control of their children today as they were in 1960. Perhaps it is asking a lot of a young single female to control her children's behavior. The crime statistics in the ghetto tend to bear this point out. Many ghetto kids leave school early to pursue street life in an underground economy, dealing drugs, committing crimes, and so on. Others leave to start a family or to work in lower-level service jobs. Are these two paths the only alternatives? If a young black person really wants to pursue a skill or vocation, schools abound in urban cities. There is also plenty of money, in the form of loans or outright grants, for those with low incomes. These avenues of upward mobility have existed for years in the ghetto, and many black youths have taken advantage of them.

During the War on Poverty era in the 1960s and 1970s, a virtual flood of educational programs hit the ghetto; many still exist. Despite these educational opportunities, many ghetto blacks opt for street life. Why? Is it racism or attitudes that are the controlling factor? I think it is attitudes, and until this painful truth is faced head-on, we will not be able to solve the problem. For example, arguing for an increase in money for education will not help those blacks who drop out of school unless somehow the value of education can also be inculcated in them. Specifically, how do you change an underclass person's values so that she or he is willing to defer gratification for long-range goals? Only a person who is willing to defer gratification will be able to pursue higher education or learn a vocation.

If Professor Wilson and other black scholars are right when they say that the deindustrialization of America's urban centers has helped create a ghetto underclass, then the only way for ghetto blacks to obtain jobs is to be better educated. Unless these blacks learn the middle-class value of pleasure deferment, pursuing a trade, vocation, or any higher educational goals will not be possible. Attitudinal changes are not easy and will require a major effort on the part of this group. All people who have successfully moved into the middle class have made sacrifices. They have deferred things they would rather do in order to work or study. It is clear that the black middle class will have to take a greater hand in helping to reverse this ghetto underclass dynamic. But they will do so not by providing excuses for ghetto lifestyles, but by confronting those lifestyles. Should I tell my children, "Since you are black, it's OK if you don't try too hard; it's OK to be a failure"? I won't accept this attitude in my own children, so why should I go before the media and provide excuses and alibis for this attitude in other children?

Last, black America needs to truly believe that it is OK to be black, that we can succeed in America without entitlements. We must believe that feelings of inferiority and incompetence are shared by all people, no matter of what race. Once black people believe that we are as good or as bad as any other people, we won't need to blame all our insecurities on racism. We, not something or someone else, will be in control of our own destinies. Less emphasis will be placed on affirmative action or minority set-aside programs as the cure-all. Who knows? We may not need them at all.

CHAPTER THREE

The Price of Affirmative Action

Affirmative action has long been a sacred cow of the civil rights community. Yet affirmative action has always exacted a price from its beneficiaries, a price which has sometimes appeared to be as high as the supposed reward. It is this "price" that I plan to discuss in this chapter. And it is this price which many civil rights advocates are loath to discuss. At the outset, I would like to say, by way of confession, that I am the product of an affirmative action program at the University of California at Los Angeles (UCLA). I confess to being an affirmative action student at UCLA in the same manner as did professor Stephen L. Carter in *Reflections of an Affirmative Action Baby*. Carter, now teaching at Yale Law School, states that he was admitted to Yale Law School because he was black. I was admitted to UCLA for similar reasons. Actually the scenario, in my case, is more complicated than that.

Carter was an excellent undergraduate student at Cornell University before he ever applied to Yale. Yet, as he says, he might not have been admitted to Yale Law School if he had not been black. My undergraduate career was not as distinguished as Carter's. In fact, my situation smacks of a

Horatio Alger story. I dropped out of high school at sixteen and finally got my diploma from Los Angeles Adult High School. I then attended a community college, where I was not exactly an exemplary student. I made it to California State College, a four-year college, only by the skin of my teeth, but I was highly successful there during my last two years. When I applied to UCLA's graduate school of political science in 1968, I had excellent grades in political science, but modest scores on the Graduate Record Exam. I was admitted anyway, and I have often wondered if I would have been admitted if I had been a white student with a similar background. I guess I will never know. I excelled at UCLA and had a highly successful graduate experience. I benefitted from affirmative action by being admitted to a major university with a full scholarship. The price I paid and even continue to pay is a sense that perhaps I did not belong at the university. As Professor Carter states in his book, I, too, will always wonder if I could have been successful on my own, without help from some "special minority program."

Many proponents of affirmative action would argue that the "price" I paid was low, considering I got into UCLA and was ultimately successful in obtaining my Ph.D. Yet they will never know how it felt or feels to sit next to non-affirmative-action students and wonder if they see you as their intellectual equal. Even more important, you wonder if you are their intellectual equal. The fear of "not being smart enough," which haunts all students, becomes even more pronounced for you, as an affirmative action student, because you didn't get there on an equal playing field. What would be the response of black college basketball players if affirmative action became a goal of the National College Athletic Association and each team had to have a certain number of white players? More important, how would the white players who joined the teams under those conditions feel? Would they feel equal to the black players? Most people believe that if two athletes compete, all things being equal, the better athlete will win. However, affirmative action, as it worked for Professor Carter, for me, and for countless others did not say that the "best" would win, only the best black. How good is the best black student? Is he or she as good as the best white student or only the average white?

While most blacks stop short of opposing affirmative action outright, an influential few suggest that the concept needs rethinking. Outright quotas, the flash point of white opposition, are increasingly rejected as counterproductive because of how whites administer them. Says Larry Thompson, deputy general counsel of Wall Street's giant Depository Trust Company, "Most of us who have benefitted from or participated in minority recruiting would be against numerical goals and quotas because all they lead to is taking the first 10 dark faces that walk through the door instead of taking people who are qualified."[1] Most important, preference programs seem to have only a minimal effect on breaking the cycle of ghetto poverty. As Professor Carter argues in his book, "What has happened in black America in the era of affirmative action is this: middle-class black people are better off and lower-class black people are worse off. . . . The most disadvantaged black people are not in a position to benefit from preferential admission."[2]

On the other side of the argument are liberal social commentators, like Stanley Fish, who believe in the utility of affirmative action. Fish argues that the objection to affirmative action denies the historical racism and discrimination that blacks have suffered. He rejects the position put forth by opponents that if it was wrong to treat blacks unfairly, it is wrong to give blacks preference and thereby treat whites unfairly. In a 1992 article entitled "Reverse Racism or How the Pot Got to Call the Kettle Black," he wrote, "This objection is just another version of the forgetting and rewriting of history. The work is done by the adverb 'unfairly,' which suggests two more or less equal parties, one of whom has been unjustly penalized by an incompetent umpire. But blacks have not simply been treated unfairly; they have been subjected first to decades of slavery, and then to decades of second-class citizenship, widespread legalized discrimination, economic persecution, educational deprivation, and cultural stigmatization. They have been bought, sold, killed, beaten, raped, excluded, exploited, shamed, and scorned for a very long time. The word 'unfair' is hardly an adequate description of their experience, and the belated gift of 'fairness' in the form of a resolution no longer to discriminate against them legally is hardly an adequate remedy for the deep disadvantages that the prior discrimination has produced. When the deck is stacked against you in more ways than you can even count, it is small consolation to hear that you are now free to enter the game and take your chances."[3]

Yet as Shelby Steele stated in a 1991 *Time* magazine interview, "Any time you have one group of preferred people and another group of unpreferred people, you are laying the groundwork for racial tension. [Preferences] stigmatize blacks in the workplace and in universities. They make black people wonder if they would be there if not for the color of their skin—wonder whether they have the competence to really compete with whites."[4] As an English professor at California's San Jose State University, Steele has emerged as the most eloquent proponent of this view. He asserts that affirmative action has reinforced a self-defeating sense of victimization among blacks by encouraging them to pin their failures on white racism instead of on their own shortcomings. Says he, "Blacks now stand to lose more from affirmative action than they gain."[5]

Many blacks have decidedly mixed views about the effectiveness of affirmative action. According to recent Gallup polls, 77 percent feel that minorities should not receive preferential treatment to make up for past discrimination.[6] But even Steele and Carter are not opposed to some form of affirmative action. The reason for the ambivalence blacks feel toward affirmative action is the mixed results one sees from such programs. For example, how would one evaluate the following two cases of affirmative action at work? In one case, for Mignon Williams, aged forty-two, a black marketing executive in Rochester, New York, affirmative action meant opportunity. She was recruited by the Xerox Corporation in 1977 under a pioneering plan to hire women and minorities and rose from saleswoman to division vice-president in just thirteen years. While Williams attributes her success mainly to hard work and business savvy, she acknowledges that her race and her sex played a role in her rapid rise. Affirmative action, she says, "opened the door, but it's not a free pass. If anything, you feel like you're under a microscope and have to constantly prove yourself by overachieving and never missing the mark."[7]

However, for Roy V. Smith, aged forty, a black eighteen-year veteran of the Chicago police force, affirmative action means frustration. Since 1973, court-ordered hiring quotas and the aggressive recruitment of minorities have expanded black representation on the 12,000-member force from 16 percent to 24 percent. Smith contends, however, that gender and race have not opened doors for him but shut them. Ironically, he has been denied promotion to sergeant so that Hispanics and females who scored lower on exams could be given the higher-ranking positions set aside for those groups. In a strange role reversal, Smith is in a position similar to that of white officers and perceives himself to be hurt by affirmative action. Last fall he joined a reverse-discrimination lawsuit against the City of Chicago by 313 police officers, mostly white. "I am not anti-affirmative action," he says. "I am just against the way it is being used. It's something that started out good and now has gotten out of hand."[8]

Smith's situation was inevitable because there are other groups that also have legitimate grievances regarding representation on Chicago's police force. And when you start to make hiring or promotional decisions based on race—or, in this case, on race and gender—someone has to lose. The losers, like Smith, are not going to be happy and will feel discriminated against.

The cases of Williams and Smith reflect an increasingly acrimonious debate among African Americans about the effectiveness and desirability of affirmative action. On one side of the argument, a small but widely publicized group of black neoconservatives contends that efforts to combat racial discrimination through quotas, racially weighted tests, and other techniques have psychologically handicapped blacks by making them dependent on racial-preference programs rather than on their own hard work.[9] In response, some scholars, like William Julius Wilson, wonder whether socioeconomic class ought to augment race, or even replace it, as a criterion in affirmative action. Proponents say that would be fairer and, in a society of limited resources, more effective. They add that it might diminish backlash, especially if preferences went to poor whites as well. Stephen Carter is far from alone in perceiving affirmative action as primarily a middle-class boon. Larry Thompson, of Wall Street's Depository Trust Company, who has recruited for his college, Yale, and his law school, Berkeley, says prestige institutions fared far better in the 1960s and 1970s in empowering the poor. Now, he argues, they enroll the children of black alumni.[10] This outcome, too, was, I believe, inevitable because these institutions want those they enroll to be successful, and who better than the children of alumni?

Princeton admissions dean Fred Hargadon allows that prestige schools are not finding enough of the disadvantaged, black or white: "None of us are yet so successful with affirmative action that we can spread resources to other social problems."[11] Whatever the best universities and largest corporations do, however, affirmative action programs are fated to remain distant from the problems of the ultrapoor. Says Eleanor Holmes Norton, a former chairman of the U.S. Equal Employment Opportunity Commission, "Affirmative action is now essentially a tool for getting people better jobs rather than for bringing the economically excluded into the system." This results from what economist James Smith, author of a U.S. Labor Department study on the problem, labels a "proskill bias." Most such programs operate at colleges and graduate schools or in private business. By the time impoverished blacks are of an age to deal with these institutions, many of them have been overwhelmed by a combination of inadequate schools, troubled homes and neighborhoods, an environment of drug use, and other social ills. Even those with the will to work often need remedial training far beyond any corporate internship.[12]

College recruitment has proved to be of limited value unless accompanied by tutoring and counseling to help disadvantaged students all the way through. Since 1976, according to Reginald Wilson, who tracks minority affairs for the American Council on Education, the share of black high school graduates attending college has dropped from 35.4 percent to about 30.8 percent, as opposed to 38.8 percent for whites, primarily because of higher dropout rates for blacks. "The tragedy on many campuses," says Wilson, "is that recruitment of minority students gets a lot of attention but remedial programs necessary for them to succeed do not."[13]

I found this lack of support for remediation also to be true at Rutgers University, and I discuss this issue as well as the decline of the black college student later in this chapter. This mixed bag of affirmative action in education also exists in other race-specific programs, such as so-called minority set-asides.[14] My father-in-law, who has run a general contracting business in Los Angeles for forty years, believes that minority set-asides only hurt black contractors. He says that there is a stigma attached to these kinds of contracts which makes it harder for a "minority" business to move into mainstream contracting. According to him, "White businesses always wonder if you got the contract because you were good or a minority." Many civil rights leaders would call this response by white business to affirmative action set-asides "racist." Yet the minority-owned firm is at a disadvantage in trying to prove that it obtained the contact on merit, not just race. Many beneficiaries of affirmative action largess have this basic lingering doubt about competence. Why was I chosen instead of someone else? If

I was hired solely because of race, what does that say about my basic worth and competence?

When I sat in my UCLA political science graduate classes, I always felt a slight uneasiness, a feeling that perhaps I didn't really belong there. To my absolute amazement, many of my white colleagues expressed similar doubts about their ability to "make it" through the graduate program. Over the years, since leaving UCLA, I have come to believe that this feeling of "incompetence" is a natural feeling, shared by many in academic life and elsewhere. However, those who came into the academic process through traditional ways had been validated numerous times along their journey. They competed openly with all others and were given no particular advantage. Affirmative action beneficiaries have not been validated in this manner and have actually suffered nonvalidation by being admitted or enrolled into a program for one reason: race.

A QUESTION OF FAIRNESS

Is affirmative action fair? Does it benefit one group at the expense of another? The answers to these questions depend greatly on how affirmative action is practiced. In situations where race or gender are taken into consideration along with other factors in making a hiring decision, it may be entirely fair. In the field of higher education, admission practices vary from college to college. To make an enrollment decision, the University of Southern California (USC) places a great deal of weight on previous members of one's family's having been students. If your father or mother went to USC there is a good chance you will be admitted, given good grades and admission test scores. Is that fair? Well, obviously USC thinks it is. This tradition of admitting the offspring of alumni is not new or unique. Most of the Ivy League colleges have practiced such admission standards.

The question of fairness is therefore a complex one. Is race a less legitimate admission criterion than being offspring of alumni? Should grades and admission test scores be the only admission standard? Harvard University receives large numbers of applicants who have either perfect or nearly perfect grades and test scores each year. Yet Harvard has tried to take into consideration factors other than academic scores as admission criteria. For example, Harvard likes to have a geographical mixture of students. Also, students with extracurricular activities will be given additional consideration. Harvard, like many other top learning institutions, believes that a "good" student is made up of more than just all A's and perfect Scholastic Aptitude Test scores.

When race is used as only one criterion among many to select students, the fairness issue becomes somewhat less critical. However, when race is the main criterion, then fairness becomes a concern. When race is the only criterion, affirmative action can be a nightmare. During my academic days at Rutgers University, I saw the down side of affirmative action admission standards. Rutgers wanted to admit black students and in doing so lowered its standards. Many of the black students admitted during this period were hopelessly behind the other "regularly" admitted students. I had black students in my classes who could neither read college-level books nor write essay examinations. The university appeared reluctant to make the financial commitment it would take to bring these students up to college-level standards. While Rutgers did provide some remediation for these students, it was not nearly enough. So, many of these students were allowed to languish and struggle in regular academic classes. As I said earlier, I had my share of these affirmative action students, and I found myself in a serious dilemma. How could I conduct a class at the college level without failing most of the black students? Should I lower my grading standards to accommodate these students or make the material easier? If I lowered standards, I would hurt all my students and do everyone a disservice.

I decided not to lower my standards, but to try to bring as many black students up to college-level work as possible. This was no easy task and required a very large commitment on my part. Even so, many of my black students could not be brought up to college-level work within the time frames and contexts that we were laboring in. Many black students failed and went home without college degrees. Was it fair to these students to bring them into college, only to fail them? I think not. But today many black college students with poor precollege credentials are failing because they have been placed in institutions with inappropriately high academic standards. Like my Rutgers students, some specially admitted black students tend to have difficulty keeping up with the normal course work.

AFFIRMATIVE ACTION AND THE DILEMMA OF BLACK COLLEGE STUDENTS

Has affirmative action caused the racial crisis on today's college campuses? Black students seem to be segregating themselves from white students in all aspects of campus life, from dormitories to the cafeteria. Why is this occurring? Recently, black writer and college professor Tamar Jacoby interviewed eighteen undergraduates—thirteen blacks and five whites—from an Ivy League college to gain some insight into their attitudes about themselves, race, and other issues. In an article, "Psyched Out: Why Black Students Feel Torn," she states, "The black students' attitudes toward 'success' were noticeably different from their white peers." Jacoby attributed the attitudes of the black students to growing up under affirmative action. She believed it had had a marked effect on their sense of standards and assessments of themselves. Some (black) students doubted that colleges bend standards to admit minorities. "This university would not risk its reputation," one youth asserted, "by putting its stamp of approval on unqualified students. I think blacks and women probably have to be better than whites to get in here." Jacoby describes a black young man who had just won a prestigious scholarship: "He came up to me after class. 'I have to admit,' he said, 'when I first learned about it, I did wonder if it was because I'm black.' But like several of his classmates he had found a way to cope with his misgivings, dismissing them as just so much unhealthy 'self-doubt.'"[15]

Jacoby felt these students were in denial and stated, "Still others took this denial a step further, until they began to doubt the very concept of merit." Finally, what Jacoby found the most disturbing was that many of the black students seemed ill at ease with their own achievement, as if it were somehow a betrayal of their race. Several admitted that they had kept their high school grades secret in order to avoid charges that they were "selling out." One premed student describing having to watch herself when she went home to Brooklyn: "If I speak in complete sentences, my girlfriends accuse me of putting on airs." She and others not only felt alienated from friends and family but were also scared that mainstream success would somehow kill what was most authentically black within themselves. "We have to figure out how to play the game," said the same young woman, "without being swallowed by it. That is the dilemma every black pre-professional has to face."[16] Jacoby said this comment prompted a chorus of amens and a long discussion of ways to counter the threat of assimilation, everything from sporting corn-row braids to making time for volunteer work in the ghetto. Despite the rather sad commentary on "success" thinking by these students, it does raise an interesting debate about the attitudes blacks have about being black. Is being uneducated, using incorrect English, and being a street person being black? Is that the standard all blacks ought to aspire to?

Shelby Steele offered an interesting discussion on being black in a 1993 interview in *People Weekly*: "Because in the last 25 years, being black has been equated with being a victim. We have a victim-focused black identity. And the higher someone moves in society, the less black they become. This becomes so absurd that I frequently hear Colin Powell's blackness questioned by other blacks. I never hear the blackness of the crack dealer in Harlem questioned. We ought to be saying that Colin Powell is the real black. The cat who's selling crack, he's not a real brother. He's an Uncle Tom, because he's harming his own people."[17]

As a child in grammar school, I can remember trying not to be "too smart" so my friends would accept me. My mother was very strict regarding using correct English in our home. But when I went to school, I would purposely use incorrect grammar to fit in with my friends. Is affirmative action responsible for making black students particularly hypersensitive to intimations that they do not measure up to the intellectual capabilities and achievements of their white peers? How great is the disparity between white and black students on some college campuses in admission criteria? In an 1993 article called "Affirmative Discrimination," Leno Graglia stated that at the University of California at Berkeley, white applicants to the freshman class need at least 7,000 points out of a possible 8,000 on an academic index that takes into account grades, honors, and SAT scores to have a 50 percent chance of admission. Black students applicants needed only 4,800. Graglia went on to discuss the continuing lag of black scores on standardized admission tests with those of whites.

These disparities in admission standards have caused some lively debates and lawsuits as well. One widely known case is that of Allan Bakke, a white applicant who had to take his case all the way to the U.S. Supreme Court to enter the medical school of the University of California at Davis. Bakke's test scores were superior to those of the specially admitted minorities. Bakke had a percentile score of 96 on the verbal section of the Medical College Admissions Test, 94 on the quantitative section, 97 on the science section, and 72 on the general-information section. The corresponding averages for the specially admitted (minority) students were 46, 24, 35, and 33.[18] Clearly the minority students had far lower scores, yet does this prove that all special admission standards are misguided and that only straight merit should be used? Not necessarily.

Another, more recent affirmative action debate took place at George Washington University over admission standards for black students. Timothy Maguire, a white law student, created a huge controversy when he published an article in the student newspaper entitled "Admissions Apartheid," in which he charged that black students were not as qualified as white students because they had lower

Law Scholastic Aptitude Test (LSAT) scores and lower grade-point averages than their white counterparts. Yet Maguire's own admission to law school had been under a special program for low testers. He admitted later that he had been admitted to the law school even though his own LSAT scores were lower than the law school's median. Maguire had been admitted because he had served in the Peace Corps in Africa; this service had given him additional points. Actually, Maguire's admission to George Washington University is an example of a good college admissions program because it is flexible and takes into account criteria other than grades and test scores. In terms of admissions to four-year colleges, it might be better for black students who are not well prepared for college to do what I did and go to a community college for two years until they are ready for a four-year college. Perhaps after two years, no affirmative action program would be needed for them to enter the university as a regular admission. Stephen Carter makes a case for limiting affirmative action to education and for holding its beneficiaries to the same standards as everyone else. I tend to agree with Carter and don't believe all affirmative action programs are bad. Those programs in education make the most sense because they can be designed to be administered fairly.

WHY ARE THERE FEWER BLACK COLLEGE GRADUATES?

In fact, fewer and fewer black college students in America are graduating. From 1979 to 1985, while the number of whites receiving bachelor's degrees remained steady, the number of blacks getting college diplomas declined roughly 6 percent. In a 1987 article called, "Why Fewer Black Students Are Graduating," Ronald A. Taylor found that blacks who finish with advanced degrees are much more rare: "Barely 11 were awarded doctorates in engineering last year (1986); only three got Ph.D.'s in computer science."[19] And the dropout rate of affirmative action students continues to be extremely high. Current figures from the U.S. Department of Education show that blacks and Hispanics are twice as likely as whites and Asians to drop out for academic reasons. In a 1991 piece called "Sins of Admission," Dinesh D'Souza stated that a recent study "of 1980 high school graduates who entered four-year colleges found that only 26 percent of black and Hispanic students had graduated by 1986. Even taking into account other factors for leaving college, such as financial hardship, the data leave little doubt that preferential admissions seriously exacerbate what universities euphemistically term the 'retention problem.' An internal report that Berkeley won't release to the public shows that, of students admitted through affirmative action who enrolled in 1982, only 22 percent of Hispanics and 18 percent of blacks had graduated by 1987. Blacks and Hispanics not admitted through preferential programs graduated at the rates of 42 and 55 percent respectively."[20] Also at Berkeley, despite aggressive recruiting, one in four blacks graduates, compared with 2 of every 3 whites. "Black students don't feel they have a place at the university, in the classroom or outside it," says Regina Freer, president of Berkeley's African Students Association.[21]

One reason why fewer blacks are coming out of colleges with degrees is that until quite recently fewer were going in. During the early 1980s, even though most colleges were trying to increase their minority enrollment, the number of blacks in four-year institutions was on the decline. The U.S. Department of Education figures show that between 1982 and 1986 black enrollment in private colleges, particularly among males, fell 5.4 percent and black enrollment at public institutions fell 4.6 percent. During that same time, the number of white students stayed about the same, while enrollment of Hispanics increased 11 percent and that of Asians 34 percent.[22] In a more recent 1990 study, the Department of Education reported that this decline had reversed itself and from the fall of 1986 to the fall of 1988 black enrollment at private colleges increased by 7.1 percent, but only 0.2 percent at public colleges.[23]

While many welcome this reversal in the decline of black college enrollment, there is still some concern over the continuing lag of black male enrollment. In 1990 the American Council on Education found that 60 percent of black students in higher education were women.[24] Why are there more black women than men in college? Dr. Troy Duster, a sociologist at the University of California at Berkeley, feels that this difference is due to differing attitudes: "Poor black men were more likely than poor black women to be influenced by 'macho' attitudes, and that those attitudes made it likely that they [males] would be driven into crime."[25]

The decline of black college enrollment during the early 1980s was not evident at black colleges. In fact, these colleges experienced a steady growth. Officials of the United Negro College Fund stated in a 1990 report that their schools had a 10 percent increase in enrollment, and that increase was equal for both men and women. These black colleges are also more successful in keeping black students from dropping out of college once they enter.[26]

In *Blacks in College*, Barnard College psychologist Jacqueline Fleming found the dropout rate at black colleges to be much lower and that about two out of three students graduate. Fleming notes that these schools enroll only 16 percent of America's black students but award 40 percent of degrees to blacks. She goes on to say that black colleges suffer from money shortages, old facilities, low admission standards, and faculties depleted by raids of corporations and major universities. Still, she concludes, "Students in black colleges seem to have a virtual corner on intellectual satisfaction." Students at black colleges, she says, build ties with fellow students and faculty members and don't feel estranged.[27]

Nearly every university is seeking ways to encourage black achievement. At state colleges and universities in Maryland, black seniors who excel meet weekly with younger blacks who are struggling. But many educators say what is needed more is a stronger commitment at an earlier level—in high school or junior high. One program widely reported on in 1992 was at the University of Minnesota in conjunction with the St. Paul public schools, which spent $2 million to single out talented minority students as early as the seventh grade and prepare them academically and psychologically through high school for rigorous college work. Another such program that I am familiar with is at the University of California at Riverside, which runs a Saturday academy for black students. The students meet every Saturday morning and learn various subjects concerning African American history. The main emphasis is to build positive self-esteem. If a student completes the entire program, which lasts several years (including maintaining good grades in regular school), they will automatically be admitted into the university.

These kinds of programs, many believe, will be the bridge that blacks need to cash in on the promise of higher education. To do without a bridge, says John Bracey, an Afro-American studies professor at the University of Massachusetts at Amherst, is "to push off into deep water from sinking sand."[28] If these early intervention programs were rigorously used, there would be no need for affirmative action because blacks could enter institutions on their own. Ironically, the only institutions where affirmative action is not practiced and blacks appear the happiest are the traditional black colleges. Black colleges like Florida A & M exert tremendous effort to make sure that those black students they admit will also graduate.

AFFIRMATIVE ACTION IN THE WORKPLACE

The concept of affirmative action was first proposed during the Kennedy administration, but it was actually put into place by the Nixon administration. As president, Nixon beefed up the Office of Federal Contract Compliance Programs, which, along with the Equal Employment Opportunity Commission, has become one of the government's two main enforcers of affirmative action policy. It oversees 225,000 companies, with a combined work force of 28 million, that do business with the federal government. In 1971, Nixon's Labor Department started the Philadelphia Plan, a quota system that required federal contractors in Philadelphia, and later Washington, D.C., to employ a fixed number of minorities. These have come to be known as set-asides and have attempted to increase job opportunities for blacks. Yet it is not clear if these quotas or set-asides have actually increased the numbers of black businesses. But what they have done is touch off complaints from many whites that blacks are benefiting from reverse discrimination.

A great deal of the anger is aimed at so-called race norming, in which scores on employment aptitude tests are ranked on different racial or even gender curves. This race norming is, in fact, what happened to our black police officer, Smith, who was passed over by women and Hispanics in the Chicago Police Department, discussed earlier. While Smith scored higher, he was ranked lower than Hispanics and women. To give an example of how ranking works, on one reported test a white applicant had to score 405 out of a possible 500 points. To get the same ranking, a black had to score 335 points. Along with the negative connotations of getting the job with much lower scores, it is difficult to argue that this is fair. The federal government regularly uses ranking for veterans, but most would agree that those who have served their country should be given some benefit over those who have not. However, being black, Hispanic, or a woman is not the same; being advanced because of this status is not generally accepted as being fair.

IS AFFIRMATIVE ACTION NECESSARY?

The black middle class has grown appreciably in the last quarter century, along with black representation in prestigious schools, high government offices, the most lucrative professions, and the military command. The extent to which the gains are attributable to affirmative action is, however, a matter of controversy. As Thomas Sowell has often pointed out, at the time that racial guidelines and timetables began to be widely enforced, around 1970, educated and well-off

blacks were already making rapid progress in various do-
mains. Still, there is no question that in the era of affirmative
action the black middle class expanded and prospered. But
if affirmative action is only a full-employment program for
the black middle class, a middle class that would prosper
anyway, then the question has to be asked: Is it necessary?
Even the strongest black advocates of affirmative action
concede that it is not a perfect tool. Like Shelby Steele, they
decry the widespread view among whites that virtually all
blacks who are hired, promoted, or gain admission to elite
colleges are less qualified than their white counterparts.

"There have been casualties, minority kids who are
depressed or feeling incompetent because of the stigma,"
says sociologist Troy Duster of the University of California
at Berkeley. Duster tells of a black student who complained
to him, "I feel like I have AFFIRMATIVE ACTION stamped
on my forehead."[29] But for most blacks, the opportunities
that affirmative action affords outweigh any potential psychological threat. Many reason that once they are on the job
or in the classroom, their performance can erase negative
stereotypes. Yet faced with white opposition and their own
misgivings about affirmative action, a growing number of
blacks would prefer to moot the argument by expanding
opportunities for all Americans, whatever their color. They
believe that instead of fighting for a fair share of the crumbs
of a shrinking economic pie, blacks should concentrate their
energy on making the pie big enough to guarantee a slice for
everyone. That would require improving schools so that
every child could obtain the skills needed to be competitive
in the labor market, a thriving economy that could provide a
job for everyone who wants to work, and more access to
capital markets for the poor and minorities who want to
start their own businesses.

This is the position advocated by William Julius Wilson, who has recently argued that race-specific programs will not garner the support they once did. Professor Wilson believes that, politically, blacks must support entitlement programs that benefit all low-income people. Only then will such programs be considered fair. Could this mean affirmative action for poor whites? Perhaps so, if these programs were structured to address solely the economically disadvantaged. Meeting these tasks might be more difficult than parceling out opportunities according to a racial formula, but in the long run they could be more worthwhile.

CHAPTER FOUR

Crime and Punishment

In 1993 nationwide, 25 percent of black men between the ages of fifteen and thirty-five were involved in the criminal justice system—as prison inmates, defendants, parolees, or probationers. In cities like Washington, D.C., the number approaches 40 percent. Homicide is now the most common cause of death for black men between the ages of twenty and thirty-five, and one in every 22 black men can expect to be murdered.[1] Every two years more blacks are killed in our streets by each other than all the black servicemen killed in Vietnam. Many liberal scholars argue that America is an inherently violent society and that criminal behavior has grown more rampant over the years. They point to the rate of violent crime, which according to 1993 FBI crime statistics was up 29 percent since 1986. Between 1986 and 1993, murder rates were up 23 percent and robbery rates had risen 33 percent. These crime rates included an absolute increase of 50 percent for bank robberies, 38 percent for street robberies, 27 percent for convenience-store robberies, 16 percent for residential robberies, and 11 percent for gas-station robberies. Aggravated assault was also up 28 percent.[2]

But what is unique about these statistics and what liberal scholars don't want to talk about is that this crime wave has been confined almost completely to black juveniles. While the arrest rates for other groups like Asians, Native Americans, and Hispanics have remained almost flat over the same period, it has risen for blacks. What is more depressing is that violent blacks are getting younger and younger. In an analysis of the *1990 Uniform Crime Reports*, James Alan Fox, dean of the Northeastern University College of Criminal Justice, "found that crime rates were up the steepest for the youngest groups. Arrest rates for murder climbed 121 percent for 17-year-olds, 158 percent for 16-year-olds, and 217 percent for 15-year-olds. Even 12-year-olds were up 100 percent."[3]

In a 1993 article called "Is Police Brutality the Problem?" William Tucker discusses this unprecedented crime wave among young blacks, which has hit cities hardest. Minneapolis, for example, has 40 percent of Minnesota's crime, even though it has only 8 percent of the state's population. New York City is another city hit hard by crime, registering 85 percent of the state's record 2,200 murders in 1990, yet having less than half the state's population. And, says Tucker, within New York City, 70 percent of the murders were concentrated in mainly black and Hispanic neighborhoods like Washington Heights, Harlem, East Harlem, the South Bronx, East New York, and Bedford Stuyvesant. Brooklyn's Seventy-fifth Precinct (East New York), with a population of 160,000, had more murders than Buffalo, Rochester, Syracuse, and Albany combined (total population 880,000).[4]

What part does racism play in these depressing statistics? Can all this be blamed on a racially biased criminal justice system? While the criminal justice system appears to be racially biased against blacks, particularly in likelihood of conviction and length of sentence, this bias does not explain the sheer number of young blacks who enter the system. FBI statistics show that black males commit a disproportionate number of serious crimes, and most of these crimes are against other African Americans. Why does this occur? Clearly part of the reason is the sociology of ghetto life, which takes many of its values from youth gangs. Black youth gangs are criminal organizations that commit much of the street violence in our urban cities. But until quite recently most civil rights organizations and liberal scholars have seemed more concerned about charging the criminal justice system with racism than about condemning black street criminals. A good example is a recent book, *Unequal Justice: A Question of Color*, by Coramae Richey Mann, an African American professor of criminology at Indiana University. Professor Mann is an acknowledged expert in the field of criminal justice, and her review of the published literature on this controversial question is exhaustive and contains a well-stated argument for the racism thesis. Professor Mann claims that the racist criminal justice system of today has been implemented by the white male capitalist elite to "maintain its hegemony" since the "means of economic and political control" used in the past "are no longer morally acceptable."[5]

She maintains that the goal of the racist system today is to "warehouse" blacks and other minorities in prison and to expand the "criminal justice enterprise" so as to provide jobs for the majority group in the law industry (law enforcement officers, probation officers, and lawyers) and in the construction industry. In short, she presents a quasi-Marxist conspiracy thesis suggesting not only that the system is racist but that it is intentionally so, as part of some grand perpetual plan to subjugate minorities. But Mann's argument is typical of those of black liberal scholars in regard to black negative behavior. Even when condemning black criminal behavior, the black civil rights community sends mixed messages about where it stands regarding crime. This grand conspiracy theory is articulately stated in a 1992 article by Les Payne called "Up against the Wall: Black Men and the Cops." In this article, Payne never addresses the issue of young blacks committing crimes but sees the problem as one of police brutality: "Police brutality toward Blacks, on the contrary, has its own cruel logic once you understand the racial history behind it. Plutarch described how the ancient Spartans used to control the Helots by weeding out the most spirited young men as a lesson to the others who would follow them. There is a similar rationale behind the excessive force police routinely inflict on African-Americans. It is part of a historical pattern of harassment and humiliation most brutishly manifested in the slave whippings and the lynchings commonplace during the first half of this century and intended to keep Blacks submissive."[6]

Payne and other black leaders believe police brutality against blacks is meant to dampen the pressure for social change by identifying potential black leaders in early childhood and diverting them to the reform school, the prison, and the grave. Payne states later in the article, "In weeding out the most aggressive, courageous and intelligent Black youngsters, the state now, as it was then, is supported by the school system, the cop, the warden, and, all too often, well-meaning parents."[7] In considering the above statistics regarding the rise in crime in urban cities, Payne and other blacks who believe as he does must live on another planet! Those "intelligent black youngsters" he is talking about are often gang members, and they are committing atrocious violent acts against other blacks. These crimes are so vicious and widespread that it caused even the Reverend Jesse Jackson to comment, on November 27, 1993, "There is nothing more painful for me at this stage in my life than to walk down the street and hear footsteps and start to think about robbery and then look around and see it's somebody white and feel relieved. How humiliating."[8]

What caused Jackson to make this comment was a series of events that occurred in his neighborhood and to his family. On August 27, 1991, four months after Jackson had moved his family into a new home in a once nice part of Washington, D.C., Jackson's mother-in-law, Gertrude Brown, was alone in the house and doing laundry. While she was doing the laundry, unbeknownst to her a burglar had entered the house and stolen a radio and some jewelry. Mrs. Brown saw someone in checkered pants running from the house. "When somebody breaks into your house and robs it," Jackson remarks, "you just feel as if everything has been breathed on."[9] Eight months later, Jackson's wife, Jacqueline, was in the kitchen early one morning as her family slept. Leaving the house to take a bag of garbage to the curb, she noticed under the streetlights three blacks, two men and a woman. She heard the woman encourage the first man to shoot the second. The second man ducked behind a dumpster. A shot was fired. The second man staggered down the street and collapsed. What was even more upsetting to Jackson was the fact that this was black-on-black violence. When a robber shot a grocer in a small store across the street, Jackson "refused to allow his wife and kids to shop there anymore," recalls longtime aide Frank Watkins. Then, on November 3, 1993, Jacqueline Jackson heard some commotion down the block and joined her neighbors outside, only to find that three young men had been gunned down in the back seat of a car by two young men who had been sitting in the front.[10] Jackson's response to this violence was to start a crusade against black street violence and crime. But in doing so, he put even more pressure on the Washington, D.C., police department.

In response to this citizen pressure, some police departments have been accused, and rightly so, of brutality in the black community. They sometimes do overreact and unfairly stop black youths. But look at the staggering problem they confront in the ghetto. The police are called by blacks to respond to crimes committed against them (blacks). If crimes weren't occurring, the police would not be on the scene.

The reason many in the black community focus on police brutality rather than on black crime is to pass responsibility onto others. As has been stated earlier, this is the common "victim" theme. Rather than blame those black youths who are committing crimes, they make the problem police brutality and the criminal justice system. In fact, for some blacks, the "victim" mentality is so strong they are reluctant to find fault in the behavior of any black person, no matter how blatant the behavior. The black civil rights establishment staunchly defended Marion Barry, the mayor of Washington, D.C., who was filmed on video smoking crack cocaine in an FBI sting operation. Before he was caught in that hotel room with a woman (she was an FBI informant) who was not his wife, rumors had swirled around him for years in regard to his possible drug use. Yet, when he was caught, not only was he defended by large segments of the black community, but he was eventually reelected as the Washington, D.C., mayor.

What makes Barry's actions any less condemnable than those of your average everyday street criminal? Barry was defended for two reasons. The first is his membership in the civil rights establishment. The second has to do with his being black and therefore being portrayed as a victim. The excuse for Barry was that he was "entrapped" by a racist federal justice system that targets black politicians for persecution. Nothing in this defense was said about Barry's voluntarily going up to the hotel room with a woman (he was married) and engaging in outrageous behavior. Did the FBI hold a gun to his head and make him smoke the cocaine? The Barry case is only one of a number of examples of the black community's closing ranks and supporting individuals who do not deserve its support.

A notorious example is the Rodney King incident, which helped spark the 1992 Los Angeles riots. No one can defend the Los Angeles police who viciously beat King while he lay helpless on the ground. The beating scene was widely televised, and two of the four officers were eventually convicted—in federal court (a state court jury found three innocent of all charges and a fourth officer innocent of all but one charge, which the jury could not decide). However, Rodney King was no hero either. First he was speeding and refused to stop when signaled to do so. He kept driving at a high rate of speed even though he was being followed by a large number of police cars. When King finally stopped, he got out of his car and refused to cooperate with officers who were trying to handcuff him. By his own admission, he had been drinking and hadn't stopped because he was on parole and afraid of violating that parole.

The police were wrong because they decided—at least the four officers did—to administer a little "sidewalk justice" by beating him until he gave up rather than just putting the handcuffs on him. If the police had done the right thing and effected an arrest the way they had been trained to do, Rodney King would have gone to jail that night, and the officers would have gone back to their duties. Can there be anything in Rodney King's actions that night to make him a hero? Several months after the Los Angeles riot, King was asked to speak at a local junior high school. He was treated like a hero by the black community. But why? What had he done that was heroic? At best, King was a victim that evening of police brutality. While the officers who beat King were wrong and at least two of them are currently serving time at a federal penitentiary, King is no hero either.

Yet as outrageous as it is to make Rodney King a hero, so is it completely incomprehensible to make the 1992 Los Angeles rioters heroes. The Reginald Denny incident is even more bizarre than the Rodney King affair. Denny, a white truck driver, was severely beaten during the first hours of the Los Angeles riot. He was driving through South Central Los Angeles when dragged from his truck and nearly killed by an angry mob. One of the perpetrators was Damian Williams, who was shown on videotape hitting Denny in the head with a brick. Williams was tried with two other rioters. Williams was also shown on the videotape spray-painting the genitals of an unfortunate Hispanic man who was also beaten by the raging mob and left for dead (a black minister is credited with saving this man's life by shielding him from the mob).

The demand of a very vocal segment of the black community was to free the rioters, the rationale being that the officers who beat up King had been acquitted (in the state trial), so these young men should also be acquitted. In actuality Williams and the others were found guilty of lesser charges. But this is not the point; what I found astounding was that so many blacks gave their support to and thereby sanctioned this criminal behavior. Many blacks, mainly leadership types, were conspicuous by their silence. Suppose Denny had been black and the mob white? What kind of outcry would one have heard coming from the black community? All those black civil rights leaders who remained silent during the Denny trial would have been shouting from the rooftops.

There is a fundamental issue of fairness in regard to how many black people view justice. It often appears that the black community demands justice for its own but is more than willing to look the other way when it comes to justice for others, the rationale being that black people are victims and should therefore not be held to the same standards as others. Damian Williams and Marion Barry are forgivable because they are black. Yet others in similar situations are not. No wonder there is such cynicism among young gang members about what is and what is not acceptable behavior when they see the black community rising in support of a Damian Williams or a Marion Barry. What possible moral arguments can be made against street gang activity when the black leadership and the black community are busy alibiing and excusing criminal behavior.

POLICING INNER CITIES

The black community sees itself as being a victim of white police. Ironically, the police who work in those areas also see themselves as victims. They see themselves as under siege in a hostile environment, with no friends. The relationship between police and community is a love–hate one, in which the police are damned if they do and damned if they don't. The police are accused of responding too slowly to calls in the black community, but when they do come quickly and in force, they are accused of overaggressiveness. Police officers are trained to respond to "suspicious" people and to be aggressive or proactive in fighting street crime. This is considered "good" police work by the police department. I did research some years ago on the Oakland police department, and using a paradigm obtained from the famous sociologist Talcott Parsons, I developed a theory of how police officers are trained. Officers are trained to respond to certain types of individuals. These "types" of individuals could be called those who fit a criminal profile. Criminologists call those who fit this profile an *ideal type*. Young black and Hispanic males fit this type, as do white youths who look like "bikers," but young women of either race usually do not. Rodney King fit this "ideal type" profile. According to the testimony of the police on the scene that night, King was a big man, muscular in build like many ex-convicts who spend a lot of time lifting weights in prison. The cops feared King. They felt he might be on a drug known as PCP, which is a stimulant and can create great strength in those who use it. The stage was set for the officers to overrespond in the King case because of how they are trained. When confronting an "ideal type," like a Rodney King, police are trained to be suspicious and to act aggressively. But what the police consider "good" police work in combating crime is considered "harassment" by many members of the black community. There is an inherent conflict between police and the black community which will be solved only when both sides get together and define their goals.

What does the black community want from its police force? And what does the police force want from the black community? First, what the black community wants from the police department is a more sensitive force that treats all fairly and with dignity. But a police force of this type is hard to come by because of the siege mentality many big-city police departments operate under. With drug traffickers heavily armed and more than likely to fire away, many officers adopt an us-against-them mind-set and a strict ethic against "ratting" on fellow officers. "If their authority is threatened, they retaliate with a kind of street justice," explains former New York cop William Walsh, a justice expert at Pennsylvania State University.[11]

Citizen demands for tough-guy law enforcers can subtly encourage intimidating tactics, too. In New York City, police recruits spend seven hours a day for eight days training with their weapons; by contrast, they devote fifteen hours over five months to racial and cultural "sensitivity" training. The police see work on inner-city streets as a domestic Vietnam, a dangerous no-win struggle fought by confused, misdirected, and unappreciated troops. They are racking up impressive arrest and imprisonment statistics without effecting much change in the situation on the street. Increasingly, police feel trapped between rising crime rates and an angry citizenry demanding immediate solutions to intractable problems. The seriousness of the problems for the police is highlighted in a previously cited article by William Tucker, which shows that murders in New York City totaled 1,077 for the first six months of 1990, up from 837 for the first half of 1989. Chicago's total—406 murders—was up 21 percent.[12]

Cops are under more pressure today then ever before. In America's Beirut-like inner cities, cops are asked to be peacekeepers among street warriors, buffers between frightened black neighborhoods and young black criminals (who commit much of the violent urban crime), and social workers for families chronically in crisis. An example of how police are being asked to minister to whole communities came in several cities just recently when a curfew for those under seventeen went into effect. Police were given the power to lodge criminal charges against parents whose children repeatedly stayed out after 11 P.M. on weekdays and after midnight on weekends. The police were asked, in this situation, to act as parents and to do what the real parents of these youths were either unwilling or unable to do.

Undergirding the enormous increase in street violence in the inner cities is the explosive potential for racial strife. While most big-city police departments have increased integration in the past generation, it is still often the case that white cops who live in the suburbs are patrolling minority communities. These officers often have little in common with the citizens they must serve and protect. "The bulk of police forces are white males of the middle class," says Ron DeLord, head of the Combined Law Enforcement Associations of Texas. "Yet we send them into large urban centers that are black and Hispanic and poor, with no understanding of the cultural differences, to enforce white, middle-class moral laws. Doesn't that create a clash?"[13]

Law-abiding black residents of crime-infested neighborhoods are desperate for police protection. They, after all, are the ones most likely to fall victim to muggers or drive-by shooters. But they also want the police's use of force kept in check, especially in poor neighborhoods where everyone is apt to be treated like a suspect. Even though so many police departments have abandoned the official use of so-called drug-dealer profiles (which is another form of the "ideal type" I spoke about earlier), officers may continue to carry racial stereotypes in their heads. To them, virtually any young black male with a gold chain is a potential drug courier. Any well-dressed black man in an expensive car might be a big-time dealer. As a result, middle-class blacks, including celebrities like actor Blair Underwood, one of the stars of the TV show "L.A. Law," complain that they have been harassed, and worse, during simple encounters with the law.

A 1991 University of Massachusetts at Boston conference sponsored by the American Civil Liberties Union (ACLU) attracted 500 people to discuss the topic of police and local communities. "Over and over, black youngsters stood up and talked about how scary and demeaning it is to be stopped and searched," said ACLU state executive director John Roberts. "Even good kids now see police as the enemy. They shun cops."[14] In some cities, relations between black communities and white cops have worsened in recent years after highly publicized incidents of police brutality or shootings by police have taken place. The response to exploding crime in some areas has been to call for more troops. However, many law-enforcement experts believe the cops' ability to affect crime rates is limited. "We're asking the police to deal with social conditions by applying laws, and you really cannot correct conditions by applying laws," says former New York City cop James Fyfe, now a professor of justice, law, and society at American University.[15]

A 1990 article called "Cops under Fire," by Gordon Witkin, found that some cities which have added police in recent years, like Phoenix and Los Angeles, have actually seen the number of reported crimes go up. In Atlanta, reported crimes jumped from 67,171 in 1987 to 88,536 in 1989, even as the number of police went from 1,346 to 1,518.[16] It is much more often the case, though, that police are being asked to do more with less. Witkin cites a U.S. Justice Department study which showed that big-city police departments employed about 2.3 officers per 1,000 residents in 1987, compared with 2.4 a decade earlier; over the same period of time, crime climbed by 22 percent. Cleveland's force had dropped from a high of 2,456 officers in 1971 to 1,661 in 1990; the city's crime rate, meanwhile, was 35.6 percent higher in 1990 than it had been in 1971.

William Tucker's previously cited study shows that despite near-record crime levels, the New York City police department had 6,200 fewer officers in 1993 than during 1970, even though the addition of 5,300 civilians to get cops out of desk jobs and back on the street had taken up some of the slack. Meanwhile, despite population losses in many big cities, calls for police service have remained high or have even increased, especially with the proliferation of 911 emergency numbers. New York police responded to 2.7 million calls in 1980; in 1993, they answered more than 4 million.[17] In some cities, it is an unwritten police policy that minor incidents like purse snatchings have to be put aside, lest they take cops away from more serious crimes. At 2:30 A.M. one summer Saturday, police in the South Dallas police district had eighty-three calls backed up. Some nonemergency calls were not answered for ten hours. By then, the incidents were over, the assailants had disappeared—and the callers were furious.[18]

Police departments are also in a losing war against drugs. In Dallas, where Sergeant David McCoy first worked narcotics years ago, he was mainly confronted with marijuana on the streets. However, when he returned to drug work in 1988, "the difference was like night and day. Cocaine was everywhere. People carried it around in candy dishes."[19] The 1980, 1988, and 1993 FBI *Uniform Crime Reports* show that nationwide, drug arrests by state and local police forces jumped from 559,000 in 1981 to 1,155,200 in 1988, and to over 2 million in 1993. But despite recent claims of progress in the drug war by federal officials, many cops and city dwellers are hard pressed to see any effect.

Drug profits have also made the lure of corruption more tantalizing than ever. "Ten or 20 years ago, when you talked about a bribe, it was a $20 bill in a matchbook," says Sheldon Greenberg, associate director of the Police Executive Research Forum, which studies police issues. "Today, you have people in the drug culture saying, 'There's 10 grand in the bag, and it's yours if you let me go.' "[20] In California, seven members of the Los Angeles County sheriff's narcotics squad went on trial in 1992, charged with skimming $1.4 million in seized drug money. In 1994, New York City held a series of hearings that exposed widespread police corruption in relation to drug sales and distribution.

Today's inner-city cops have also seen the resurgence of street gangs, many of which profit from narcotics and enforce their own ruthless brand of law with drive-by shootings and turf wars that leave the law officers ducking for cover. The Crips and the Bloods, originally Los Angeles street gangs, have now spread to more than 100 cities and total more than 40,000 members, according to the FBI. And cops say the modern-day bad guys seem more willing than ever to tangle with the law. "You used to go to a party and say, 'Break it up,' and they would break it up," says Cleveland detective Robert Zak, a twenty-five-year veteran. "Now they throw beer bottles at you and smash the windows of your patrol car."[21] Cops also worry about the appearance in recent years of high-powered, rapid-fire weapons like MAC-10s and Tec-9s, which spew up to thirty rounds in a minute. No one keeps track of gun sales nationwide, but production figures illustrate the trend; street criminals today want 9-millimeter semiautomatic pistols that reload quickly and carry more bullets.

Recently, the Clinton administration was successful in having certain assault weapons outlawed, but the gun industry had already put millions of such weapons on the streets. It's not that more cops are killed these days, but the attitudes, the weapons, and the unpredictable stimulant effect of crack have created a volatile mix that leaves cops feeling more vulnerable. In addition, many cops are frustrated by rampant gunrunning, which renders even the toughest local gun-control laws virtually useless. New York City, for instance, has one of the nation's strictest antigun measures, so weapons needed by criminals there are simply purchased in states with little regulation, like Georgia, Texas, Virginia, and Florida, and then driven north to New York. Gordon Witkin cites an analysis of 315 guns seized by New York police in 1990, which showed that 79 had been bought in Virginia, 60 in Texas, and 30 in Florida. Only 15 had come from New York. One exasperated Bureau of Alcohol, Tobacco, and Firearms agent complained that "half the guns in Brooklyn" came from a single gun store in Richmond, Virginia.[22]

POLICE BRUTALITY

Much has been learned in the past generation about how to curb police abuse, and many departments have tried to apply those lessons. One problem appears to be the reluctance of some police agencies to weed out the relatively small number of repeat offenders who are responsible for much, if not most, police abuse. Over the last few years there have been frightening incidents of police brutality. Gordon Witkin gives examples of several police brutality cases that have occurred over the years: In 1991, five New York City officers were indicted on murder charges in the February 5 death by suffocation of a twenty-one-year-old Hispanic man suspected of car theft. The officers were accused of having hit, kicked, and choked Federico Pereira while he lay face down and perhaps hog-tied—his wrists cuffed behind his back while another set of cuffs bound his hands to one ankle. In Memphis, during the same year, a black county sheriff was convicted of violating civil rights laws in the June 1989 choking death of Michael Gates, twenty-eight, a black drug suspect. Gates's body was covered with bruises in the shape of shoe prints. In 1992 fifty people demonstrated outside a Plainfield, New Jersey, police headquarters, charging that a police officer had beaten Uriah Hannah, a fourteen-year-old black. According to the protestors, Hannah and his friends had been playing with a remote-control toy car on a sidewalk near his home. A motorist stopped short at the spot where the boys were playing, and a police cruiser ran into the rear of his car. Hannah's parents, whose older son had allegedly committed suicide in police custody in 1991, charged that the officer jumped from his car, accused the teenager of obstructing traffic, and at one point tried to choke him. The boy's parents were arrested when they tried to intervene.[23]

In a Miami incident that ultimately sparked disturbances in December 1992, several of a group of six policemen allegedly beat to death Leonardo Mercado, a Puerto Rican drug dealer. All had remained on patrol duty even though five of the six had previously shown up on the Miami police department's "early-warning list" for their violent behavior and three had been counseled for stress in the months before the incident. Among them, they had "forcibly controlled" suspects a total of thirty-eight times in three years. All were cleared of civil rights violation charges.[24] In Los Angeles in 1992, as I have already reported, the police beating of black motorist Rodney King sparked the worst riots in American history. Of the four officers indicted in the King beating, two had suspension records; one had been removed for sixty-six days in 1987 for beating and kicking a suspect.

Cities have an incentive, other than love of humanity, to curb abusive cops. Richard Lacayo's 1991 article "Law and Disorder" shows just how expensive police brutality is: Los Angeles paid $10.5 million in 1990 to settle civil claims, and localities from Dade County, Florida, to San Diego shelled out millions of dollars to victims during the 1980s. This cost doesn't include the cost of riots set off by police–citizen conflicts. Four riots in Miami since the early 1980s, started after police killed blacks in disputed circumstances, have led to more than $100 million in damages. The Los Angeles riot in 1992 was estimated, by the *Los Angeles Times*, to have cost $50 million and has the dubious distinction of being the most expensive riot in the history of America.

Yet the distressing truth is that brutality is likely to endure for these reasons:

1. Police brutality is hard to prove. Since most abuse occurs out of the public eye, the lack of independent eyewitnesses makes cases very difficult to prove. The Rodney King case was unique because amateur filmmakers are usually not standing by to film the incident, as happened in the King case.

2. The person abused by police typically has a criminal past, which usually causes juries and prosecutors to side with the cops. Nationwide, the U.S. Justice Department is reported to have presented to a grand jury just 2 percent of the 15,000 brutality complaints that arose in 1991. Local investigations are often less than thorough, too. Lacayo's previously cited article provides a good example of this carelessness. He reported on a 1988 Chicago case in which

civilian investigators backed an officer who said he had killed a man because the man charged him, but the investigators never checked an autopsy report showing that the victim had been shot in the back.[25]

Not surprisingly, civil service regulations and union rules help protect abusive cops. Citizens Alert, a Chicago watchdog group, says the city's police union has forced the adoption of a rule that bars investigators from consulting a cop's prior record during a probe. Meanwhile, in 1991 the *Miami Herald* reported that the civil service board had retained most of the twenty-four troubled officers that the police chief had wanted to fire since 1989, including one abusive cop who had shown up on the department's early-warning list twenty-three times in ten years.[26]

What is the answer to reducing police brutality? Aleem Fakir, who heads a black Miami civic group, believes that police departments "need to stop the fox from watching the hen-house and have more community civilian boards monitor them."[27] Also, early-warning systems that automatically subject officers to investigations after several brutality accusations can help, as does reshaping a police force to reflect a city's ethnic makeup. Lacayo reports that the decline of brutality complaints in Houston and Philadelphia coincided with the reigns of black police chiefs who stressed programs that send cops out to cope both with crime and with social problems. In Atlanta, U.S. Representative John Lewis, who as a civil rights leader was bloodied by state troopers, insists that a white-on-black beating like the Los Angeles incident couldn't happen in his city because of the large percentage of black cops on the force.

Many believe that the Rodney King case and the alleged racist remarks and laughter of the cops who beat King suggest that Police Chief Daryl Gates's history of deroga-

tory remarks about minorities created an open-season atmosphere among officers who worked the city's dangerous
night beat. In response to serious charges of racism, Los
Angeles hired black Police Chief Willie Williams to head its
force after Gates was pressured to resign. Still, all such
reforms can be virtually worthless unless the local police
chief chooses to set and enforce a tone of tolerance of minorities and intolerance of abuse. Many police agencies, for
example, have intensified formal training for recruits on
how to handle charged incidents such as the aftermath of
high-speed chases, but the training has little impact when
field commanders feel free to ignore it. Ultimately, the com-
bative nature of policing and the chronic tensions in inner
cities will ensure the persistence of some brutality. But it is
hoped that the growing and appropriate national revulsion
over Rodney King's beating will make more than a few cops
think twice before they exult about beating a suspect—or
wield their nightsticks so freely.

POLICE VERSUS THE BLACK COMMUNITY

Ultimately the police will do most of their policing in
the black community because that is where most of the calls
come from and where the crime is. Police officers tend not to
be sociologists or social workers, but today's modern cop
may have to be. In San Jose, California, it has been proven
that good policing can take place with community support.
A 1992 PBS television program showcased the San Jose department and found that the department had upgraded its
officers in terms of education to an average of two years of
college per officer. Citizens in minority communities were
heard to say, although grudgingly, that the department had

improved over its uglier past, when it was thought brutal. Yet, as was stated earlier, cops feel they are under siege. "A policeman can start out bright-eyed and bushy-tailed, but it goes away quickly on the street. It takes a mature officer not to stereotype people. Immersion into the police culture can quickly strip away a rookie's idealism," says Hubert Williams, president of the Police Foundation. "Many officers will say, the moment I graduated from the police academy my partner told me, 'Forget all that stuff they told you at the academy; this is the real world.' "[28]

Many of the best cops are no longer willing to pay the physical and psychological costs and are retiring. Partly because so many seasoned officers have retired, departments around the nation have found themselves seriously understaffed. Others have expanded too rapidly, filling their ranks with inexperienced and, sometimes, poorly trained officers. This might have happened to the Los Angeles police department, which grew from 6,282 to 8,382 between 1988 and 1991; 38 percent of its field officers and 36 percent of its sergeants had had less than three years on the force. In the end, police departments nationwide must learn constraint in dealing with inner-city crime. Perhaps lawsuits have had a deterrent effect on police overresponse. However, it must be said that the police did not create the problems of the ghetto, and yet they are called on to help solve them. Unfairly, many see law enforcement as a solution to crime rather than as a stopgap measure. Good policing will not end ghetto pathologies and is analogous to putting a Band-Aid on a cancer.

CHAPTER FIVE

Blacks, Jews, Koreans, and Hispanics in the Promised Land

It is not surprising that today's blacks and Jews find themselves in conflict. What is surprising is that the so-called coalition between blacks and Jews, which started in or around 1910 and lasted until the 1960s, lasted as long as it did. The black–Jewish coalition began unraveling during the 1960s because of the rise of black nationalism. *Nationalism*, by definition, is ethnocentric and, while more sharply defining one group's cultural heritage, tends to exclude other groups that are not part of that heritage. The black–Jewish alliance has always been a tenuous one, as Jonathan Kaufman's *Broken Alliance: The Turbulent Times between Blacks and Jews in America* (1988) so aptly points out. In fact, there was only a marginal alliance between these two groups during the period of slavery; some Jews sided with the Confederacy.

The coalition actually started when eastern European Jews started coming to America in large numbers. These Jews were more likely to be socialist in ideology and therefore more committed to the plight of workers. The rise of the Ku Klux Klan during the turn of the twentieth century put Jews and blacks in the same boat. The alliance, accord-

113

ing to Kaufman, was started out of mutual self-interest. Jews helped found the National Association for the Advancement of Colored People (NAACP) in 1896, and by the 1930s, a quarter of all black children were being educated in schools built by Julius Rosenwald, the founder of Sears.[1] During the 1960s nearly one-half of all white civil rights workers were Jewish. These civil rights workers, along with their black counterparts, rode the freedom buses throughout the South, taking tremendous risks with their safety. Two of these Jewish civil rights workers were murdered, along with a black worker, in Mississippi during this turbulent period.

Blacks and Jews probably shared their closest ties at this time, yet the rifts had already begun. As early as 1935 there was a riot in Harlem, New York, directed against Jewish merchants. The Student Non-Violent Coordinating Committee (SNCC) started to purge all its white members in 1967 in conjunction with the rise of the "Black Power" movement. Black nationalism is not easily compatible with interracial coalitions. Black nationalism in America traces its roots to the back-to-Africa movements of Martin R. Delany during the 1860s and Marcus Garvey in the 1920s. Delany was a free black who had once tried to get into Harvard Medical School but was denied. He was a brilliant man and became the first black to serve as a captain in the Union Army during the Civil War. Marcus Garvey was a West Indian–born black activist who headed a popular back-to-Africa movement during the 1920s. Both Garvey and Delany before him were black nationalists in their views. After the Civil War, Delany explored several plans to repatriate blacks in Africa. The famous black orator had this to say about Delany: "When I get up in the morning, I thank God that I am a man. When Martin Delany gets up in the morning, he thanks God he was born a black man."[2]

Black nationalism can be equated in some sense with

Zionism—not the Zionism that believes in the formation of a Jewish state, but the Zionism of the late Rabbi Meir Kahane, who argued that Arabs have no place in that Jewish state. I heard Kahane also say, during a television interview, that he felt Jews had done too much for blacks and should concern themselves only with helping other Jews. But what Kahane and black nationalists like Louis Farrakhan fail to understand is why blacks and Jews got together in the first place. Historically, organized racist groups in America have hated not only blacks, but Jews as well. These racist groups have tended to lump both groups together, perhaps because of the earlier coalition between blacks and Jews. The reasons for the coalition therefore are still relevant today. David Duke, the ex-Nazi white supremacist who ran for governor of Louisiana, is anti-Semitic as well as antiblack. Many blacks, not being students of the Holocaust, have a hard time seeing Jews, who are white, as a legitimately oppressed group. So when Jews speak about anti-Semitism and racial hatred, many blacks do not take them seriously.

Perhaps a certain amount of envy of Jewish successes is involved in the rift between blacks and Jews. Certainly, to the extent that blacks see themselves as chief victims, there is little room for others to take on this role. Except for lingering anti-Semitism, Jewish oppression worldwide is mainly historical. It would probably be helpful to the black community if there were more sensitivity to this oppression. This sensitivity might help rekindle some remnants of the old coalition between the two groups.

WHAT JEWS RESENT ABOUT BLACKS

Jews are disturbed by the silence of black leadership when people like Louis Farrakhan, leader of the Nation of

Islam, or Leonard Jeffries, who in 1991 caused such turmoil at the City University of New York, make blatantly anti-Semitic statements. In the case of Jeffries, chair of African American Studies at the City University of New York (CUNY), much can be said. First, Jeffries is quite openly anti-Semitic. In a 1991 article about Jeffries called "The Provocative Professor," Lance Morrow quoted Jeffries as saying during one speech, "Russian Jewry had a particular control over the movies, and their financial partners, the mafia, put together a financial system of destruction of black people. This was a conspiracy programed out of Hollywood by people called Greenberg, Weisburg, and Trigliani."[3] Morrow also quoted Jeffries as saying, "Rich Jews operating in Seville and Lisbon and Hamburg and Newport, RI, and other cities financed the African slave trade."

Needless to say, Professor Jeffries has made all these statements with little credible evidence. What concerned Jews was not Jeffries's statements, but the mild response of black leadership to those statements. Jeffries has not been publicly condemned by black leadership. In fact, Jeffries's appeal seems wider than just the CUNY African American Studies Department. He is reported to have been greeted by 1,000 supporters at the John F. Kennedy International Airport when he returned from a trip to Africa. He was also cheered at a black church by 1,000 of his followers, and his now infamous speech was played on videotape.[4]

Jews wondered where black leadership was hiding. But what really troubled organized Jewish leadership was the black community's response to Louis Farrakhan, head of the Black Muslims. Farrakhan has made many openly anti-Semitic and antiwhite statements over the years. But his most famous—or infamous—was made about Jews in 1984 and reported in a 1988 article called "Hate Story: Farra-

khan's Still at It" by David Kurapka. Farrakhan is reported
as saying, "How come the Jews don't like Farrakhan, so they
call me Hitler. Well, that's a good name. Hitler was a very
great man. He wasn't great for me as a black person, but he
was a great German. Now, I'm not proud of Hitler's evil
against Jewish people, but that's a matter of record. He rose
Germany up from nothing. Well, in a sense you could say
there's similarity in that we are rising our people up from
nothing. But don't compare me with your wicked killers."[5]

Farrakhan has made many other derogatory remarks
about Jews. In extended excerpts from his speech entitled
"Empowerment in the Black Community through Politics
and Economics," given on March 11, 1988, he said, "And I
respectfully say to my Jewish friends, please don't call me
anti-Semitic. Go and study the state of Israel. The Ashkenazi
Jews are European Jews who converted to Judaism. They
never had any roots in Palestine. They never came from
Palestine. These are Europeans who have come into Palestine and now the Falasha Jews and the Black Hebrew
Israelites, they are suffering under the rule of the real anti-
Semite, who is Yitzhak Shamir. Where are the Asiatic Jews?
Where are the African Jews? Why don't they have an equal
share of power in Israel? It is because the real anti-Semite is
in power and he clutches the Semitic people who are of
Afro, Asian, and Semitic origin, not these Yiddish and Polish
speaking people."[6] Historically, David Kurapka says, Farrakhan is wrong about European Jews. He says the origins
of European Jewry are in Palestine: "The Jews of Palestine
were expelled by the Romans in 70 A.D., and spread to North
Africa and Italy (where many were Roman slaves). And
Ashkenazic Jewry was formed, broadly speaking, by the
movement of Jews in Italy to northern France and Germany,
and later eastward, to Central and Eastern Europe. A minor

point, perhaps, but important, because Farrakhan bases his anti-Semitism on the notion that Jewish people have exploited an exaggerated misery to gain power, and his anti-Zionism on the notion that the emigration of Jews to Palestine was not a return."[7]

Farrakhan infuriates Jews when he charges that because they control the media, he has gotten bad press. He also agrees with Professor Jeffries that Jews financed the slave trade. He has accused Jews of pulling political strings behind the scenes and controlling the banks. When a relatively obscure black Chicago city official, Steve Cokely, said in 1987 "that the AIDS epidemic is a result of doctors, especially Jewish doctors who inject the AIDS virus into blacks," Farrakhan supported him, stating, "Cokely spoke the truth."[8] In fact the anti-Semitic statements by Cokely were made at Farrakhan's mosque in Chicago in November 1987. In four speeches made between 1985 and 1987, Cokely had vehemently attacked both Jesse Jackson and the then black mayor of Chicago, Harold Washington, for retaining Jewish advisers. He had alleged that Jewish physicians were injecting black children with the AIDS virus. He had denounced Christopher Columbus as a Hispanic Jew, described the cross as a symbol of white supremacy, and accused Jews of creating a "secret society," the purpose of which was to form a world government, controlled by the Jews, that would oppress blacks.

"The Jew," Cokely had stated, "hopes to one day reign forever." Many prominent black leaders expressed solidarity with Cokely on the grounds either of freedom of speech or of the truth in what he said. Not one black elected official chose to contradict Cokely. The Reverend Herbert Martin, who was a prominent black leader in Chicago, declared that he thought Cokely's comments had a "ring of truth." "They're inflammatory, yeah," Martin said. "But sometimes the truth is rather inflammatory."[9] This position by Martin and other black leaders infuriated Jews in Chicago and eventually nationwide. Why was black leadership either supportive or silent about this anti-Semitism? Because black leadership sees black people as victims and therefore as entitled to vent their rage. Jews become the victimizers even though there is not proof of any special victimization of blacks by Jews. Cokely summed up this position when he stated, "We've been slaughtered, killed, beat up, locked down 400 years and we are the victim, and we will be accused of being racist when we oppressed nobody."[10]

This thinking renders all who believe it guilt-free, not responsible for their destinies, and therefore outside the rule of law. Those who are pure victims can do anything. Perhaps the most important function of Cokely's and Farrakhan's rhetoric is the very simple one of making those who believe it feel good about themselves. Some black leadership sought to excuse Cokely's statements about Jews by declaring he didn't really "mean it in his heart." These same leaders have tried similar alibis for Louis Farrakhan. While Farrakhan's separatist and extremist group, before whom Cokely delivered his speeches, is estimated to have no more then 5,000 to 10,000 adherents, few black leaders, including Jesse Jackson, will openly repudiate his anti-Semitic remarks. Many Jews feel that, by not directly opposing anti-Semitic statements by Farrakhan, Cokely, Leonard Jeffries, and others, blacks legitimize them.

But Chicagoan blacks are divided on Farrakhan. Some, who dislike the horrible things he says about Jews, feel that they can still approve of his attacks on black drug-taking, prostitution, and lethargy. His words, they argue, cannot hurt American Jewry; his actions may be helping American blacks. As Clarence Page, a black syndicated columnist with the *Chicago Tribune*, suggests, blacks and Jews have difficulty in understanding one another because each group interprets its priorities in the light of its separate but horrendous past. American Jews focus on the importance of denunciation, recalling that it was the failure to denounce Hitler's evil that opened the way to the Holocaust. American blacks focus on the importance of unity, arguing that it was black disunity that facilitated slavery.

Last, American Jews resent black ingratitude in not recalling the part played by Jewish activists in the early years of the civil rights struggle, symbolized by the two young Jews who were lynched, alongside a black comrade, in Mississippi in 1964. But all that was a long time ago. Jewish and black paths diverged in the late 1960s, and a generation of blacks has grown up unaware of that old black–Jewish alliance. Individual Jews carry on the tradition, but for young blacks struggling up from the bottom, the Jewish community has blended into the prosperous, uncaring mainstream of white America.

WHAT BLACKS RESENT ABOUT JEWS

Many blacks feel that the Jewish community is not as free of racism as it would lead others to believe. They are quick to cite the case of Michael Levin, a City University of New York philosophy professor who wrote an article in the Australian journal *Quadrant* in 1987. Levin, a Jew, stated, "The Trouble With American Education . . . turned out to be the staggering energy expended to bring American Negroes into the educational mainstream. And the reason these costs were so staggering and why quotas won't work has to do with the fact that, 'On average, blacks are signifi-cantly less intelligent than whites.' "[11] Levin cited IQ tests which showed blacks lagging fifteen points behind whites in scores. He also cited the Berkeley professor, Arthur Jensen, who said that only 20 percent of a person's IQ can be attributed to nurture. Thus, Levin concluded, "Black under-performance is not due to white oppression therefore whites have no obligation to act affirmatively in order to close the gap."[12]

There has been a vigorous debate over the meaning of IQ scores. IQ tests do not measure all types of intelligence, and cultural bias in these tests is inevitable. Also, African Americans, because of race mixing, share phenotypically with whites a wide range of colors and racial characteristics. Do those blacks who are genetically closest to whites score higher, on average, than those who are more purely Afri-can? As one can see, there are many unanswered questions even when IQ tests are viewed as completely legitimate measures of intelligence.

But aside from this debate are the obviously racist views of Levin, who also said white shopkeepers had a right to close their doors to suspicious-looking blacks. The incon-venience to innocent blacks was no greater than that faced by whites who lost jobs to blacks through affirmative action. While it is probably not true, many blacks see Levin's views, and those of his wife, who teaches at Yeshiva University, as representative of a larger segment within the Jewish com-munity. It is ironic that both Levin and Leonard Jeffries are members of the same faculty at the City University of New York. Both represent extreme views which have taken on a larger-than-life significance. Michael Levin's views were ex-tremely hurtful and infuriating to blacks, but the Crown Heights affair created even more of a schism.

In August 1990 a little seven-year-old black boy was

killed by a Hasidic Jew. It was unclear whether the death occurred because of negligence by the driver or simply by accident. The aftermath created a frenzy of black anti-Semitism and Jewish outrage. Black mobs threw stones at Jewish homes and marched through Crown Heights. Yet some of the black anger against these Crown Heights Hasidic Jews had its roots in earlier incidents. According to a 1991 article called "Crown of Thorns: The Roots of the Black–Jewish Feud," by Jonathan Rieder, the Crown Heights Jews had started their own crime patrols. Rieder says of these Crown Heights patrols, "But when it comes to Jewish survival, such partisans of Judeocentricity are not restrained by liberal squeamishness. One guardian I met in Canarsie, [an] Orthodox Jew recalled, 'We had vigilantes in Crown Heights, and we stopped the niggers there.' "[13]

There have been incidents of Hasidic Jewish patrols stopping black youths and questioning them because they looked as if they didn't belong in the neighborhood. This has turned black sentiment against Jews. Crown Heights was only the proverbial "straw that broke the camel's back." Add to this statements by one Hasidic leader who said blacks are just jealous of Jews because "the Jewish Community works, the Jewish community is not on crack, and the Jewish community does not have single-parent families."[14] Of course, the above statements infer that all blacks don't work, do use crack, and live in single-parent homes. Blacks also resent the unqualified support American Jews give Israel. Since the early 1960s, blacks have increasingly tended to identify with so-called third-world peoples. The Palestinians are seen as a dispossessed people who are being unfairly treated by Israel. Jews see Israel as a Jewish homeland and do not agree with blacks.

Many blacks resent Jewish resistance to affirmative action. They see this opposition as racial in nature and cannot understand the Jewish argument which speaks about how Jews oppose quotas in general. American Jewish organizations have been very successful in opposing affirmative action programs. Blacks have not forgotten that, as recently as 1978, a Jewish student, Allan Bakke, with support from American Jewish organizations, won a U.S. Supreme Court case when he claimed that, because a medical school had turned him down in favor of less-well-qualified blacks, he was the victim of reverse discrimination. While some blacks see affirmative action as a ladder up, Jews see it as the ceiling beyond which they cannot go. Again, despite the merits or failings of affirmative action, neither blacks nor Jews understand each others' political priorities. Last, some black resentment of Jews is quite frankly brought about by competition for jobs and for university positions.

I think blacks and Jews still have a reason for an alliance. From the black perspective, I think that Jews are the only whites who really understand what it is like to be disliked for reasons outside one's control. And while Jews certainly don't suffer from racism or discrimination to the same extent as blacks, they can understand that discrimination historically. What blacks must do is more strongly condemn the few virulent anti-Semites within their leadership. Blacks must also accept the idea that another people—in this case, Jews—may have a history of oppression as horrendous as their own.

WHY BLACKS RESENT ASIAN MERCHANTS

The history of ethnic businesses is nothing new in the black community. Jewish merchants had a tradition of business dealings in black areas before the Watts riots of 1965 in Los Angeles. After the riots and the resulting destruction to their stores and places of business, these merchants left and were not replaced until the advent of the Korean merchants. Today, according to the Los Angeles Chamber of Commerce, 60 to 70 percent of all businesses in the black sections of Los Angeles are owned by Asians, especially Koreans. How did this come about? Better yet, why did this happen? One reason is that many blacks with the ability and resources to operate a small "mom-and-pop" business would not consider running one of these neighborhood businesses. As a black friend who owned a successful fast-food franchise once said to me, "Who would want to own a store like that with the crime rate being what it is?"[15]

The Korean merchants are filling a vacuum left by the flight of the black middle class. This phenomenon exists not only in Los Angeles, but in Chicago, New York, Philadelphia, Washington, D.C., Baltimore, and elsewhere. This Korean influx into the ghetto started because of the liberalized immigration law of the mid-1960s, which speeded up the exodus of Koreans to the United States and led to a Korean takeover of retail niches in the ghetto economy. Over the years, blacks have complained that Korean merchants do not treat them with respect. There may be some truth to this charge because of a rich vein of ethnocentrism in Korean culture and resulting racist attitudes. Chris Herlinger reported on such cultural differences in a 1992 article called "Culture Clash," citing one man who stated that even before he left South Korea, "I had the idea that blacks were dirty and aggressive from American films and from our experience with black soldiers. My very first day in America, I was afraid to go outside because of the dangerous blacks."[16]

Herlinger notes there is also a difference in cultural style. Koreans tend to shy away from direct eye contact as a sign of impoliteness, and they are not given to smiling at

customers. Avoiding physical contact with men, Korean female cashiers may drop change on the counter. At a meeting
with blacks, a leader of the Korean Produce Association
searched for commonalities: "Our Chang music is like your
soul music: it comes from the heart. Like African Americans,
we were enslaved," but added, "We Koreans have great
strength of endurance. We don't express our joy or laugh
easily or share agonies."[17] In New York, Koreans and Caribbeans have clashed over cultural differences. As one writer,
Earl Ofari Hutchinson, observed in a 1991 article called
"Fighting the Wrong Enemy," "The root cause of conflict
between the Koreans and their black customers is due to
cultural differences. Caribbeans, being used to the West
Indian market economy, like to bargain. They take their
mangoes to the register and offer less than the price, or
pluck a grape and test the sweetness of the bunch."[18]

This sort of thing, continued the writer, "drives the
merchants crazy. Some consider it tantamount to stealing."
In discussing his disgust with the Koreans, one West Indian
stated, "We never had these problems with the Jews!"[19] The
Korea Times, aware that black grievances are more than racist
fabrications, has taken to warning merchants not to put
profit above all else. Blacks complain about the scrutiny they
undergo when they shop in Korean stores. They feel that
this scrutiny presumes they are all shoplifters. The Korean
merchants complain about the large amount of theft they are
subjected to. "How do we know which ones are going to
steal?" asks a merchant. "We have to watch everybody."[20]
Some merchants simply charge off theft. One explains, "The
moment you make an issue of it, they start screaming, 'You
racist.' They make everything racial. You just try to get them
out of the store."[21] When Korean merchants try to open bags
or stop customers, they run the risk of creating an incident

such as the boycott of two Korean stores that occurred in Brooklyn, New York, in January 1990.

That incident made national news and was widely reported in the media. It started out as a dispute between a black customer and a Korean merchant. The details of the incident that triggered the boycott are murky, but according to the protesters, the Koreans "disrespected an African sister," a Creole-speaking Haitian named Jiselaine Felissaint, who tired of waiting in the checkout line and headed for the door. When she refused the grocer's demand that she open her bag, she was (allegedly) beaten savagely. The Koreans claim Felissaint paid two dollars for three dollars' worth of plantains and limes, and when the cashier requested the dollar, she retorted, "You Chinese, Korean motherfucker. Go back to your country."[22] The cashier reportedly said, "This is not your country, not my country, it's everybody's, right?" After an additional exchange of words, a tussle ensued, and the woman fell to the ground, claiming injury. Rumors circulated that the Koreans had beaten a pregnant woman, and that an elderly black woman was now in a coma. (The police and hospital reported a slight facial scratch.) The outraged crowd threw stones and bottles at the store. When a Korean took refuge in another produce store across the street, the crowd's wrath turned on it too.[23]

Through the spring, boycotters, ranging from two or three in the morning up to a few dozen in the evening, walked the picket line. Business at both stores plummeted, from thousands of dollars a day to less than $50. Korean merchant organizations pumped $8,000 a month into each store. One merchant, standing next to his empty store, was perplexed: "Why do they chant, 'Korean people must go?' If you cut your hand, the color is the same. . . . We are all the same. But they say black is black power, black is special people."[24] Across the street, another merchant asked, "How could we be rude to our customers? In this area, there are six fruit and vegetable stores. We are competing each other. This boycott is murder. This is mental killing. Why they do this to me?"[25] While the boycott was still being maintained against the Koreans in New York, an even more sinister and dangerous confrontation between the two groups occurred in Los Angeles.

On the morning of March 16, 1991, a Korean merchant, Soon Ja Du, was working the cash register at the Empire Liquor Market in South Central Los Angeles, in one of the city's poorest neighborhoods. She and her husband had bought the rundown store in 1989, hoping to run their own business and give their children a better life. Because of her fear of crime, Du was there only on weekend mornings, when it was quiet. In two years, the Dus' store had been held up three times and burglarized more than forty others. Around 9:45 A.M. that day, fifteen-year-old Latasha Harlins, a black teenager, came in to get some orange juice. She put the $1.79 bottle in her knapsack and approached the counter. According to a security-camera videotape, Latasha had money in her hand. But Du accused the girl of shoplifting, and a violent argument ensued. Du, forty-nine, grabbed Latasha by the sweater. Latasha responded by punching the shopkeeper. As the girl turned away, Du raised a pistol and fired at the back of Latasha's head, killing her. Black groups in Los Angeles led a summer-long boycott of Korean merchants after Latasha's shooting, and several Korean-owned stores were firebombed.[26]

The resentment blacks feel toward Koreans has many facets. One may be cultural differences and lack of knowledge about each other's culture. Another more profound reason is the Koreans' success. As one woman stated after the Brooklyn incident, "The Koreans are claiming buildings we've dreamed of, that we've longed for, for years."[27] Many blacks feel that once again they are being denied their place in the ethnic queue by newcomers who are leaping over them. For years, I have heard my black friends in Los Angeles say that "suddenly the Koreans are everywhere; they are taking over our neighborhoods." Some blacks believe the Koreans were given special treatment by the government and given money to establish themselves. One black woman lamented during the Los Angeles incident, "How else can poor people like that just come to this country and do that unless they have been given a fund? There's no one doing that for black people."[28]

In fact, the start-up capital for a grocery store is typically less than $10,000, and banks and the government are rarely its source. Koreans get capital from relatives, from their own labor and self-denial, and from mutual savings associations. At the heart of black resentment against Koreans is the exasperation many blacks feel because they have been unable to do what the Koreans have done. Sometimes this exasperation comes out in the form of Korean-bashing. A *New York Post* editorial summed it up when it decried "scapegoating New York's Koreans" and argued that the Korean formula of hard work and loyal families "is a path open to any group that wants to follow it."[29] The *Post* implied: Blacks fail to travel that path. Black sensitivity to the implications of Korean success was demonstrated at a black–Korean consciousness-raising session in Los Angeles when even the most moderate blacks bristled at the phrase "hard-working Koreans" and replied, "We work hard too!"[30]

Why can't American blacks emulate the Koreans? Is the Korean success due to some strange immigrant ethic? The Koreans are said to work fifteen- to sixteen-hour days, for years, to extract a profit. Another recent immigrant group, West Indian blacks, has reclaimed entire neighborhoods in New York and is also emulating the old immigrant formula of hard work. Blacks resent Korean businesses because the existence of these businesses points out a painful failure in the black community, namely: If Koreans who barely speak English can start businesses, how come blacks in the community can't?

There are two possible answers: (1) there is a lack of a entrepreneurial business tradition, and (2) those blacks who could operate a business want a more high-level business. In terms of the first point, John Selby Butler wrote an entire book, *Entrepreneurship and Self-Help among Black Americans* (1991), which chronicles 200 years of black business entrepreneurship in America. Yet, interestingly, as racial conditions for blacks improved black business enterprises disappeared. Blacks pursued other interests and agitated to move into mainstream America. As was stated earlier, the best and brightest of the black community are often not interested in small-business start-ups. David Abner III, a professor of management at Howard University's school of business, observes, that "when you look at those who go to business school, particularly as undergraduates, you're looking at people who want to get into the mainstream by going into corporate America."[31]

And in graduate school, a good percentage of blacks come from industry and are looking to advance their careers, seeking upward mobility in organizations of which they are already a part. Abner adds, "With major corporations actively recruiting minority managers nowadays," most of his best students prefer opportunities in big business to the risks and headaches of running their own small companies."[32] In other words, educated and talented blacks are busy pursuing the American dream and are not willing to re-create the immigrant experience of opening up a small business on a "shoestring" like the Koreans.

BLACKS AND HISPANICS

There are many Hispanic groups in the United States, but I discuss here mainly Mexican-Americans, Puerto Ricans, and Cuban-Americans, who make up the largest groups. Racial tension appears to be highest among blacks and Mexicans in the Southwest and particularly in California. California is a state with rampant illegal immigration and, along with Texas, has undergone the greatest increases in its Latin population. Today, Mexican-Americans (and Mexican illegals) are the largest nonwhite minority group in the Southwest. In Los Angeles, Latinos make up about 43 percent of the entire population of the city. Their conflict with blacks is of rather recent origin, but with the rising unemployment rate, there is increasing competition for jobs. Latinos are the workers of choice in the unskilled and semiskilled trades in Los Angeles. They are willing to work cheaply and in conditions that many native-born Americans are unwilling to abide. Also, for whatever reason, Latinos are less threatening, more pliable, and generally more acceptable to many employers than blacks. According to an article written in 1991 by Jack Miles, a *Los Angeles Times* reporter, "Whites are more comfortable with Latinos than blacks." He cites as evidence the hiring practices of several trades, such as construction, janitorial, and other service jobs. Miles goes on to say, "If you live here, you don't need the General Accounting Office to bring you the news. The almost total absence of black gardeners, busboys, chambermaids, nannies, janitors, and construction workers in a city with a notoriously large pool of unemployed, unskilled black people leaps to the eye. According to the U.S. Census, 8.6 percent of South Central Los Angeles residents sixteen years old and older were unemployed in 1990, but an additional 41.8 percent were listed as 'not in the labor force.' If the Latinos were not around to do that work, non-black employers would be forced to hire blacks—but they'd rather not. They trust Latinos. They fear or disdain blacks. The result is unofficial but widespread preferential hiring of Latinos—the largest affirmative-action program in the nation, and one paid for, in effect, by blacks."[33]

I think there is a feeling of being overwhelmed by Latinos in black communities. In Texas there appears to be less conflict than in California. The reasons are not clear. Perhaps the economic conditions are different. In California's major urban areas, manufacturing still flourishes because of the ever-growing source of cheap, largely illegal labor. Many newly arrived illegals will work for wages well below the market level for that job. Ironically there is also growing tension between Hispanics who are old arrivals (American citizens) and those who are new arrivals (who are mainly illegal). The old arrivals are concerned about how the local economy can absorb this staggering number of immigrants.

In July 1991, the Black Leadership Forum, a coalition headed by Coretta Scott King (Martin Luther King, Jr.'s widow), Walter E. Fauntroy (member at large of Washington, D.C.'s elected but unofficial congressional delegation), and Jack Otero (the president of the Labor Council for Latin American Advancement), wrote to Senator Orrin Hatch urging him not to vote to repeal the sanctions imposed on employers of illegal aliens under the Immigration Reform and Control Act of 1986. "We are concerned, Senator Hatch," the group wrote, "that your proposed remedy to the employer sanctions-based discrimination, namely, the elimination of employer sanctions, will cause another problem—the revival of the pre-1986 discrimination against black and brown U.S. and documented workers, in favor of cheap labor—the undocumented workers. This would undoubtedly exacerbate an already severe economic crisis in communities where there are large numbers of new immigrants."[34]

For the most part, blacks get along best with their Puerto Rican neighbors in cities in the East and the Midwest (there have been rifts, however, such as when New York State NAACP president Hazel Dukes caused outrage among Latinos in 1991 by charging that Spanish-speaking immigrants were taking low-wage jobs from blacks).[35] However, blacks get along relatively well with Puerto Ricans, compared with other Hispanic groups. The reasons for such cordial relations has to do with the lack of competition between the two groups. In fact, historically, blacks have tended to feel superior to Puerto Ricans. Puerto Ricans are some of the poorest of the poor in America. Puerto Ricans are the second-largest Hispanic group, 2.75 million people in the mainland United States. A third of them live in one city, New York. But the 1990 census data show that Puerto Ricans are the worst-off ethnic group in the United States.[36]

For a period in the mid-1980s, nearly half of all Puerto Rican families were living in poverty. And this poverty did not seem to be a function of their unfamiliarity with the mainland United States, their inability to speak English, or their lack of education. Mexican-Americans, who are no more proficient in English than Puerto Ricans, less likely to have finished high school, and more likely to have arrived here very recently, have a much lower poverty rate than Puerto Ricans.[37] The *Journal of the American Medical Association* reported in 1991 that, as the newsletter of a leading Puerto Rican organization put it, "On almost every health indicator . . . Puerto Ricans fared worse" than Mexican-Americans or Cubans. Infant mortality was 50 percent higher than among Mexican-Americans, and nearly three times as high as among Cubans."[38]

In New York City, blacks' median family income is substantially higher than Puerto Ricans' and is rising more rapidly. The black home-ownership rate is more than double the Puerto Rican rate. Puerto Rican families are more than twice as likely as black families to be on welfare and are about 50 percent more likely to be poor. In the mainland United States, Puerto Ricans have nothing like the black institutional network of colleges, churches, and civil rights organizations, and there isn't the large cadre of visible Puerto Rican successes in nearly every field that blacks have. Black politicians are more powerful than Puerto Rican politicians in all the cities with big Puerto Rican populations, and among Puerto Ricans there is the feeling that blacks have America's attention, whereas Puerto Ricans have become invisible.

Cubans, on the other hand, are the most prosperous of the Hispanic groups. They have now risen above the national mean in family income. Most Cubans reside in Miami, Florida, and their prosperity, since they began to arrive in numbers in 1965, has been phenomenal. In 1965, a six-day airlift brought 260,000 refugees from Castro's Cuba to Miami, and blacks found themselves competing with the Cubans for jobs, housing, and other opportunities. Since then, the number of Hispanics has more than tripled, to 825,000; in Miami they now outnumber blacks by 450,000.[39]

Cubans have become the dominant economic and political force in Miami. The city's first Cuban-born mayor, Xavier Suarez, thirty-nine, was elected in 1985. Blacks, by contrast, have made few economic or political strides. Since 1980, black unemployment in Dade County (Miami's county) has risen to 10.4 percent, and the jobless rate for Hispanics has dropped to 5.8 percent. While Cubans have expanded their ownership of small businesses, Miami has one of the smallest black professional classes of any American city its size.[40]

Many of the former Cuban refugees had been members of the middle class in Cuba before Castro took over. When they fled to Miami, they brought their middle-class values and background with them. The tension between blacks and Cubans in Miami has resulted in two riots in ten years. The first riot occurred in 1980 and was the result of white officers' shooting black suspects. A 1989 riot happened when a Hispanic officer shot two black motorcycle riders, killing one. But the underlying reasons for the rioting had to do with black anger, says Marvin Dunn, a black psychologist who coauthored a study of the 1980 riots: "A larger and larger segment of the black community is falling farther and farther behind the rest of us in income and in the quality of life."[41] Ironically, blacks in Miami are now faced with another influx of Hispanic refugees who will compete with them for jobs. These refugees are from Nicaragua, and as many as 200 refugees a day are hitting town. By the end of 1994 more than 100,000 Nicaraguans will have sought refuge in Miami.[42] Many blacks in Miami charge that the city goes out of its way to provide housing, jobs, and social services for the Hispanic immigrants, while ignoring the needs of the black citizenry. "The Nicaraguans get food, they get clothing," says Vanessa Haynes, thirty-four, a black data-entry officer at the University of Miami. "What do our people get? Nothing!"[43]

REASONS FOR BLACK–HISPANIC CONFLICT

I believe that the reasons for conflict between blacks and Hispanics are both economic and psychological. Much of the conflict is fueled by black resentment of being replaced by these relatively newly arrived immigrants. Further exacerbating black anger is the seeming success that some of these groups have had at the expense of blacks. A much larger question is why people who have handicaps similar to those of blacks, such as discrimination (plus language barriers), can come to America and, within a short time (a few decades), move ahead of blacks on the economic ladder. While many blacks complain that these newly arrived immigrants have got special favors from government, this argument is not true. As was pointed out earlier, the Asians pooled their money and lent it out to their own people to start businesses. In Miami, the Cubans are using the American system through voting power to achieve political power, but where have the blacks been all those years in Miami, before the Cubans got there? Rather than rage against these ethnic groups, blacks should learn a lesson from the most successful of these groups: group unity and self-help. This is the magic immigrant formula, and it can still work.

CHAPTER SIX
Welfare Dependency

Blacks are dependent on a number of government programs, not just welfare. Unfortunately, blacks have been taught early that government works. It was government—in this case, the Northern states—that ended slavery. Government made blacks citizens through passage of the Thirteenth Amendment. Government responded to black demands by passing civil rights legislation that ended legal segregation and voting discrimination. So it should not be surprising that for many blacks government intervention is essential in solving black problems. As I have argued earlier, this favorable opinion of government is unprecedented for any other group of Americans. Traditionally, black people have looked to the federal government for help when times were difficult. Black leaders, from the ex-slave Frederick Douglass to today's civil rights leaders, have asked the federal government to lend a hand to help blacks overcome social ills.

But when the issues were slavery and its aftermath, this need for governmental assistance was obviously necessary. Even during the period of legal segregation in the South, government help was essential to overturn "Jim Crow" laws.

However, this dependence by blacks on outside forces to solve black problems has, it appears, led to a certain dependency of its own. Today one can hear this rhetoric of dependency from many blacks and their leaders portraying black people as victims of society, powerless to make a change in their lives. This rhetoric of victimization and powerlessness is a self-fulfilling prophecy because powerless people, by definition, cannot bring about meaningful change. Change can be brought about only through government actions which place all black aspirations in white hands. Government is largely controlled by white people, and if they decide not to act, black hopes are doomed.

For all the negative aspects of the Black Muslims and Minister Farrakhan, they do not see themselves as helpless or as victims. Their teaching is for black self-sufficiency and reliance.

Along with this rhetoric of dependency comes the notion that all black people are victims. Cornell West, a distinguished and widely read black intellectual, states over and over again in his best-selling book, *Race Matters*, that all black people are victims. Yet West, in all his brilliant scholarship, does not seem to understand the price one pays for believing oneself to be a victim. One effect is to help condition blacks to see themselves as victims in need of assistance, as victims without responsibility for creating their own problems or obligations to solve them. Indeed, in neglecting to communicate everyone's duty to take advantage of the available opportunities, and also in constantly berating the "establishment" for not doing enough to help disadvantaged minorities, intellectuals have been sending the message that blacks have mainly rights and whites mainly obligations.

THE WELFARE DILEMMA

The central dilemma of our welfare state is the age-old general tension between "compassion" and "dependency." This dilemma stems from the central fact that so-called welfare (actually Aid to Families with Dependent Children, or AFDC) goes to women with children. For most of the able-bodied, Americans have decided against much cash compassion. Ours is a more specific and modern dilemma: What about a single, able-bodied woman who must care for a child? If we give her no more aid than we give able-bodied men, we may be punishing the child. But to aid the child, we must aid the mother, which AFDC does. But when we aid the mother, do we also risk the "social hazard" of encouraging women to put themselves in a disastrous dependent position. This is the main thesis of conservatives like Charles Murray, who believe that the AFDC system says to poor women, "Have a kid, and the state will take care of you—as long as you don't live with the father." To men, Murray believes, the system says, "Father children, and the state will take care of them."[1]

The conservative theory argues that prospective mothers and fathers are influenced directly by a certain economic rationale which enables a woman to have babies and know the state will take care of them financially. Murray in particular believes that a woman may have a baby just so she can go on welfare. Fathers leave their wives or girlfriends so that these women can qualify for the program. Believers in this theory argue that welfare caused the growth of the underclass. Charles Murray compares in minute detail, in *Losing Ground*, the financial prospects of Phyllis and Harold, a fictitious ghetto couple on and off welfare, concluding that, between 1960 and 1970, benefit increases and eased eligibility rules had tipped the balance and made welfare an appealing option. Says Murray, "as 'absent father' cases grew from 30 percent of AFDC homes in 1940 to 64 percent in 1960, even many liberals were quite willing to denounce AFDC's 'discrimination' against intact families."[2] The preferred liberal solution, however, was not to take benefits away from broken families but to extend them to intact ones, argues prominent writer Mickey Kaus in a 1986 article called "The Work Ethic State: The Only Way to Break the Culture of Poverty." The guaranteed-income concept was the logical conclusion of this line of thought. But even during the liberal 1960s, guaranteed-annual-income policy discussions were never serious.[3]

What does cause welfare dependency? Charles Murray and the conservatives think they have an answer, but their thesis, which argues that welfare availability creates more women willing to have babies out of wedlock, also has problems in terms of explaining welfare causation. If Murray's thesis is correct, one would assume that as welfare benefits decreased, so would illegitimate births. Yet the illegitimacy problem got worse in the mid- to late 1970s, even though AFDC benefits were falling in real dollars. And in a 1984 study, David Ellwood and Mary Jo Bane of Harvard University compared family structures in states with varying benefit levels and concluded that high benefits have no effect on the decision to have a baby.[4] Ghetto teenagers don't have children to go on welfare, according to Ellwood and Bane, they have babies to increase their self-esteem, to give themselves "something to love" in a world where delayed gratification seems pointless.

Murray and the conservatives have countered the above argument with two points:

1. While AFDC payments have gone down in real dollars since the early 1970s (they have not risen as fast as the rate of inflation), other benefits such as Medicaid, food stamps, and housing subsidies have made the entire welfare "package" larger than it was in the early 1970s.

2. Though welfare benefits may not have caused a teenage girl to have a baby out of wedlock, they have acted as an enabler. Welfare created favorable conditions for out-of-wedlock births and therefore the growth of the underclass. With AFDC in place, young girls look around them and recognize, perhaps unconsciously, that girls in their neighborhood who have had babies on their own are surviving, however uncomfortably.

Conservative arguments notwithstanding, I think even some liberals have begun to see welfare as an umbilical cord through which the mainstream society sustains the isolated ghetto society and permits the expansion of this single-parent culture.

The tragedy of our present welfare system is that it makes family formation economically irrational. If a man decides to take responsibility for his family and remains in the household, the woman loses a tremendous number of her benefits. Who knows how many families were never formed because of the fear of losing welfare subsidies? Yet the conservative argument is compelling because it states that, once AFDC benefits reached a certain threshold, they allowed poor single mothers to survive and thus facilitated the growth of the underclass. Welfare allowed single women to have babies for all the various nonwelfare reasons they have them. In fact, it is precisely because nobody has babies in order to go on welfare that marginally lowering welfare benefits won't stop these women from having babies.

What's the solution? Supposing there were no welfare

at all? Would things change? Charles Murray believes they would. During a debate on television, he recently stated that he felt single-parent births would go down: "You're going to have lots of single women talking differently to their boyfriends. And if they didn't, their plight trying to raise kids without welfare would serve as an example to their neighbors."[5] But Murray was challenged by black conservative Glenn Loury, a participant on the program, with this dilemma: How do we as a society allow children to suffer and not act to help them? If we act and take the children away from the mothers, where do we put them? And more important, at what cost? This dilemma has always sustained the welfare system, and unless we are willing to let children suffer as an example to others (which is Murray's goal), real change will not happen. I don't believe most policymakers and implementers have the stomach to go through with Murray's "solution" (and Murray himself waffles) and will be compelled to come up with a more humane way of changing the welfare culture.

There does remain the possibility that something less drastic than Murray's ultimate solution—to end all welfare as we know it—might work. This is the promise of the current Clinton administration welfare reforms. These reforms are a revision of the old "workfare" approach to welfare. One of the more controversial aspects of the proposed welfare "package" is the "two-years-and-out" provision. The two-years-and-out provision presupposes that other aspects of the welfare proposal already be intact, such as a comprehensive job-training program, available child care, universal health care, and jobs once the person is out of job training.

Other variations of welfare reform are also appearing in several states. For example, New Jersey has enacted a law stating that no welfare recipient will receive an increase in benefits if she has another child. The rationale for this law is that welfare recipients must plan the growth of their families just as the rest of society must and that, if they don't, then society should not have to pay. All these proposals have in common the attempt to force welfare recipients to work and to take responsibility for their own choices.

WELFARE DILEMMA:
MUCH DISCUSSION BUT LITTLE REFORM

Much literature has been written about welfare reform since the late 1960s. The problematic development of a welfare culture (or underclass) has been written about in Nathan Glazer's *The Limits of Social Policy* (1971); Martin Anderson's *Welfare* (1978); George Gilder's *Wealth and Poverty* (1981); Ken Auletta's *The Underclass* (1982); Charles Murray's *Losing Ground* (1984); and, in 1992, Lawrence M. Mead's *The New Politics of Poverty*, Daniel Patrick Moynihan's *How the Great Society Destroyed the American Family*, and Mickey Kaus's *The End of Equality*.

Improbable as it might appear, the first really radical scheme to reform welfare was proposed by Richard Nixon. In 1969, Nixon proposed an ambitious and politically left-sounding guaranteed income for families with children. His then domestic adviser, Daniel Patrick Moynihan, threw in a rather modest "work requirement" to (it was said by critics) placate conservatives. Remarkably, the Nixon plan offered the poor money with no strings attached. Thus it was the opposite of what most people meant by *workfare*, which is that welfare recipients be required to work—in government public-service jobs if necessary—in exchange for their welfare checks. The next serious attempt at welfare reform took place during the Reagan administration. Actually, Ronald Reagan first proposed a workfare program in California in 1967. He proposed a similar program when he became president in 1981. Partly because of liberal opposition, Reagan's California program never really got off the ground, but he persisted, and when he got to Washington in 1981, he proposed requiring all states to make welfare recipients work off their grants at the minimum wage. Congress didn't give him that, but it did allow the states to experiment with workfare if they wanted to.

What is surprising is the amount of agreement on welfare reform there has been among both liberal and conservative politicians. While they have agreed that work is good and welfare is bad, no one knows how to break the cycle of welfare dependency. Given the Reagan administration's mandate for the states to experiment with welfare, several states tried various reforms programs during the 1980s. Mickey Kaus, in a previously cited article, described one such experimental program: the Massachusetts Employment and Training Choices program, or ET for short. ET was not a workfare program per se, but a voluntary program which tried to persuade welfare mothers to enter training or take jobs. There was nothing mandatory about it. Welfare mothers with no children under six had to register for the program, but "It's nothing other than filling out a form," said the then Massachusetts welfare commissioner Charles Atkins.[6] Welfare mothers were offered a variety of services designed to help them find work, such as job appraisals, career-planning workshops, remedial education, job training, and placement services. Those who found jobs got transportation allowances and free day care for a year after they started work, plus Medicaid for up to fifteen months if their employers didn't provide health insurance.

But ET had no teeth. Welfare recipients didn't have to do anything to receive benefits. If the recipients refused ET's "invitation" to participate, they were placed on an automated "future participation" list and targeted for special marketing campaigns. This approach allowed them to stay home and collect a check. And of the 112,983 welfare cases in Massachusetts in 1985, only about 7,660, or 6.8 percent, actually got full-time jobs through ET. ET is an example of one of the major criticisms of previous welfare policy: It used a social work model that didn't work. The traditional liberal social-work model presupposes that when confronted with options and information people will choose the correct path. Welfare policy has always relied on this model and has believed that recipients would voluntarily leave the system once they received the necessary benefits and services. However, with the explosion in single-parent, female-dominated households, many policymakers have started to rethink the old social-work model and to opt for a stricter, more punitive approach to welfare.

Workfare was the new approach, and it has gained much popularity since the early 1980s. Workfare, unlike the old welfare approach, believes that welfare recipients should work for the benefits they receive from the state. Workfare is the embodiment of the Protestant Ethic in terms of believing that "work" itself has value, even if the work is menial. The proponents of workfare do not believe that welfare recipients will voluntarily get off the system. They argue that if society could rely on welfare recipients to end the culture of poverty by working themselves out of it, there probably wouldn't be a culture of poverty in the first place.

Workfare proponents believe there are people who won't climb up a "ladder of opportunity" even when the economy or the government dangles it in front of their noses. Unlike in the social work approach, workfare supporters hope to bring about dramatic change by making people do things they might not do if they had a check coming every month. Workfare says that, if you take the state's money, the state has a right to ask something in return. If you choose not to work, then you receive no benefits. It's as simple as that.

During the 1980s, many states experimented with various forms of workfare. Everyone was enthusiastic about this new "get-tough" attitude, except for one problem: It didn't work. Many of the state workfare programs had problems. The mandatory work provisions of their programs were not so mandatory after all. Some maintained large "unassigned pools" of recipients who were receiving welfare but not working. Illinois, for example, ended up doing little more than providing recipients with a "modified job search component," in which it contacted the recipient "at least" every six months. San Diego's workfare program "required" new applicants to perform public service work, but once applicants had been excused for health or other reasons or had obtained an exemption, they did not have to work to receive benefits. Most state workfare programs have been largely ineffectual. West Virginia, for example, had one of the toughest welfare programs, but it excused welfare mothers from work when they were "job-ready" (because working off their grant couldn't teach them anything more) or when they had "barriers" to employment. And in 1986 that let off the hook 20,000 of the then 36,000 participants.

Some state programs required welfare recipients only to show up for twelve or thirteen weeks of "work experience." Other states had glorified job-search programs in which recipients learned how to write a résumé, dress for an interview, read the want ads, and then actually look for jobs under the prodding of supervisors. These attempts were also largely ineffective in dramatically reducing the welfare rolls. In actuality most of the programs billed in the press as "workfare" during this time were really mandatory job-search schemes with a short "work experience" requirement at the end for those who didn't find a job.

While several states have lately started to take a harder approach to welfare reform, none has yet applied a truly mandatory work requirement to their entire caseload. California has a program which tries to make work mandatory. It is called GAIN (Greater Avenues for Independence) and tries to impose a mandatory program on the largest welfare caseload in the country. California's plan offers a generous menu of training and education "options" to welfare recipients in addition to "work experience." The work experience option has been defined differently in different parts of California. In Riverside County (a place I am familiar with since I live there), welfare recipients are strongly urged to go to work as soon as possible. Riverside hired job scouts who got recipients jobs in the private sector. This saved the taxpayers in Riverside $2.84 for every $1.00 spent in their welfare costs.[7] Other counties in California allow their welfare recipients a choice: They can take vocational education, remedial education, or English as a second language, among other programs, instead of working for their checks. Though GAIN, in theory, has tried to require all recipients to do something, no recipient would be forced to work off her grant right away. If the recipient doesn't get a job after training in a specific job skill, then the state may require her to work off her grant, but it must offer her a workfare job that uses the skill she has learned. Welfare mothers trained as nurses' aides cannot be required to work as secretaries, and so on.

As a strategy to destroy welfare dependency, GAIN suffers from the two major structural flaws common to most such programs. First, it requires nothing of welfare mothers until their oldest child reaches the age of six. This one restriction excuses two-thirds of the welfare caseload in California. Second, if anyone wants to avoid the workfare obligation all she has to do is go home and have another baby. This is what California state senator Diane Watson threatened her inner-city constituents would do when confronted with what she called "forced labor."[8] One way around this possible loophole is to extend workfare to mothers with no children younger than three, which would bring 62 percent of the national welfare caseload into the program. This is in fact one of the many proposals currently on the table regarding welfare reform.

Another issue that neither GAIN nor any mere workfare plan addresses is how to get fathers involved in the financial support of their families. States like Maryland, Missouri, and South Carolina are seeking to require the establishment of paternity for children before a mother can receive AFDC benefits. Establishing paternity would allow the states to go after fathers for some support for their babies. However, if fatherhood is encouraged along with intact families, something must be done for fathers who do not have competitive skills or jobs. Some have suggested that offering women who head fatherless families a way out of poverty through workfare, while failing to offer it to potential fathers (or childless women), may reinforce whatever incentives in favor of single-parent families the AFDC system generates.

BLACKS, LIBERALS, AND WELFARE REFORM

Black civil rights leaders and white liberals have been slow to jump on the welfare reform wagon. For many black leaders, black people are an oppressed victim class in America and welfare is an earned entitlement. Today, even these leaders have started to feel uneasy with the increase in out-of-wedlock births reaching 60 percent and the likelihood that a permanently dependent black underclass is developing in America. Both white and black liberals have come to the realization that welfare reform is necessary. In fact, in order to find someone who publicly discounts welfare reform, one would have to visit a member of the old left in America and read Richard A. Cloward and Frances Fox Piven's 1993 article "A Class Analysis of Welfare." Cloward and Piven are famous social scientists who have written extensively about the poor and public policy, and in this article they said, "The program we call welfare provides a bare subsistence income to four million women raising children. It costs $22 billion dollars, much less than 1 percent of the federal budget, and only 2 or 3 percent of most state budgets. Yet this small program has become the focus of big intellectual and political guns. Liberals and conservatives agree that welfare is our big problem, bad for the country, and bad for the poor. Presumably, it drains public budgets and reduces work effort. And by allowing poor mothers to opt out of paid work, it saps their initiative, and nourishes the cultural and psychological disabilities attributed to the 'underclass.' As a result, welfare is said to worsen poverty. The proposed remedies vary, but they usually involve cutting benefits and pushing mothers into the labor market."[9] Cloward and Piven believe that the real reason behind welfare reform is to weaken labor by forcing low-wage workers

into the workplace. They see a conspiracy between big business, which wants cheap labor, and politicians, who are
willing to provide that labor by driving people off welfare.
Welfare provides an "escape valve" for exploited labor and
frustrates big business because it does provide unskilled
labor with a choice—of not working.[10]

Cloward and Piven go on to argue that the expansion of
income maintenance programs in the late 1960s and early
1970s insulated wages from the effects of rising unemployment. The extension of social security coverage, together
with higher benefits, sharply reduced workforce participation by older people. At any one time, 3 million women were
on the AFDC rolls in the early 1970s, and few of them were
then required to participate in welfare-supplemented work.
The expansion of the disability programs from less than 1
million recipients in 1960 to more than 4 million in 1975 also
produced a sizable drop in labor force participation, since
many of these people were of prime working age.

The increase in the welfare rolls, say Cloward and
Piven, greatly concerned the economic elite in America,
who began to recognize that income maintenance programs
(like AFDC) had weakened capital's ability to depress wages
by the traditional means of intensifying economic insecurity.
In effect, social programs altered the terms of the struggle
between capital and labor. To stop this trend and return low-
wage workers to the business elite, an all-out effort was
launched to restore labor discipline by slashing the income
support programs, including placing large numbers of AFDC
women in the labor market with welfare supplementing
their low wages ("workfare"). Programs, especially those
that reached more vulnerable groups, were badly damaged,
and even unemployment insurance coverage was severely

restricted. Welfare and food-stamp grant levels fell sharply, and eligibility for benefits was restricted. Nearly a half a million people were removed from the disability rolls. Cloward and Piven cite a series of studies of the food stamp program—by the Urban Institute, the Congressional Budget Office, and the General Accounting Office—which found that only one-third to one-half of all eligible persons were receiving food stamp benefits. And an Urban Institute study reported that one-third of those eligible for Medicaid, a health insurance program specifically for the poor, were not receiving benefits.

But, say Cloward and Piven, the main focus of discussion by politicians and policy intellectuals has always been the welfare program. They go on to say, "It is easy to see why. Welfare, with its ancient connotations of pauperism and its contemporary association with blacks, could easily be made to symbolize the error of the very idea of income support programs. And welfare recipients—most of whom are single mothers, many of whom are minorities, and all of whom are desperately poor—could easily be made to symbolize the failures of character of those who drop out of wage work. Welfare clients always suffer the insult of extremely low benefit levels, and are always degraded by the overbearing and punitive procedures of welfare agencies. Now, as public furor over welfare builds, meager benefits are cut, and degrading procedures multiply. The moral for Americans who are working more and earning less is clear. There is an even worse fate, and even lower status, than hard and unrewarding work."[11]

In their arguments against welfare reform, most black leaders and white liberals do not go as far to the left as Cloward and Piven, but many of these leaders are still not wholeheartedly behind welfare reform. For example, in President Bill Clinton's 1994 welfare reform bill is a provision that recipients be off welfare in two years. To accomplish this goal, the bill calls for some public sector jobs if the recipient is not able to get a private sector job. This provision is controversial for two reasons: First, it will force the recipient to leave welfare within a certain time, and second, it may cost a lot of money to provide welfare recipients with public sector jobs. Making the reform even more unworkable, it seems, is the proposal by liberal Congressman Harold E. Ford, who chairs the House Ways and Means Subcommittee on Human Resources and recently demanded that all community service jobs pay $9.00 per hour. Another provision of the Clinton proposal is the family cap which forbids parents on welfare from getting increases in benefits if they have another baby. The National Organization for Women's Legal Defense Fund spokesperson, Martha Davis, says of this proposal, "It is crucial to expose the racism and sexism of the reformers."[12]

Not all black leaders follow this antireform approach. New Jersey lawmaker Wayne R. Bryant, a black Democrat from Camden, helped to write a reform law which does not allow a welfare mother to get increased benefits if she chooses to have another child. The law also requires young welfare mothers to stay in school and maintain average grades. Says Bryant about welfare, "Welfare is a modern day form of what I call slavery. . . . It is a destructive force for low income families."[13] Yet blacks and liberals are still fearful of some of the Clinton proposals. Congressman Barney Frank, a liberal Democrat, said recently, "I don't think he'll [Clinton] sign a bill . . . unless there are alternatives to cutting people off entirely."[14] But what good is any sanction if it is never used?

THE LOW-WAGE DILEMMA

What is the low-wage dilemma? The dilemma is simply that the sort of jobs welfare recipients can get in the marketplace will not support a mother with kids—so that any decent welfare standard will pay more than most potential jobs. This problem has always troubled any true reform, but it is changing. In a 1994 article, Marshall Ingwerson states that more than two-thirds of the states have proposed or are already making changes that allow welfare families to earn more and save more without losing their AFDC. Generally a family receiving AFDC cannot save more than $1,000 or own more than $1,500 of equity in its car. Earnings on a job can reduce welfare benefits dollar for dollar earned, so that it is not practical to work. Today, twelve states have raised limits on savings and earnings. States like Maryland and New Jersey have proposed raising the asset limit to $5,000. The vehicle limit is $15,000 in New Jersey and has been removed entirely in Maryland.[15] Raising the earnings limit causes some fear because for every person it gets off welfare, another is likely to get on. But the alternative to raising earnings limits is the status quo, which means there is little incentive to get off welfare because the recipient loses so much.

HOW TO END WELFARE DEPENDENCY

Welfare dependency will never be ended without some pain on the part of the recipients. Change is difficult for most people, and they change only when it is absolutely necessary. Welfare dependency is more than just lack of employment opportunity; for some it has become a way of life.

Females who head fatherless households are hard-core unemployed. Many have never worked a day in their lives,
and if they have, it has been at the most menial of jobs. To get
jobs, these women will need a great deal of courage and
enthusiasm to overcome the fear of getting out there and
"putting themselves on the line." The world of work is a
scary place for those who have never been in it. Getting a job
is harder, in many respects, than working because of the
rejection one encounters in job hunting. The only way that
long-term, hard-core welfare recipients are going to enter
this world is if they are compelled to do so. Why? Because,
as I said earlier, people find it hard to change. With this in
mind, what should be the goal of welfare reform?

I agree with the conservatives who believe that the goal
ought to be the long-term destruction of welfare dependency. If this is the policy, it becomes unimportant whether
sweeping streets or cleaning buildings helps a welfare
mother learn skills that will help her find a private sector
job. What is important is that the work ethic be enforced and
that the mother do something to earn her benefits. If she
learns competitive skills along the way, so much the better.
Maybe if welfare mothers knew in advance that they might
have to perform menial labor to work off their grants, they
would think twice about having an illegitimate child and
dropping out of school and onto welfare. Those who champion work requirements think it's good when welfare
mothers work off their grants, whether or not working increases their income. If she is still working for her grant two
years or ten years later, it's still better than not working. Says
Lawrence Mead, who wrote an influential book in 1986
called *Beyond Entitlement*, "If she learns some skills while
sweeping and cleaning, if it motivates her to go get a private
sector job, that's gravy."[16]

There is also the issue of fairness. A great many Americans work in dead-end jobs. According to Columbia University labor market expert Eli Ginzberg, 40 percent of the jobs in the economy are "bad jobs" paying low wages and offering little chance for advancement. Yet these Americans are not subsidized by welfare payments, nor are they provided with free education and training. But will the possibility of having to work off a grant in a public service job provide an incentive for welfare recipients to take a "bad" private sector job even if it's not required? In the past, states with generous welfare benefits like California required a private sector job to pay as much per hour as the welfare benefit. Very few jobs that welfare recipients qualified for would pay wages that high. Today these ridiculous rules are changing so that welfare recipients will have to take jobs. A more thorough discussion occurs next.

WHAT WORK WILL THEY DO?

There is the pernicious question: What will the workfare workers do? Many answer that question by saying that America's infrastructure needs repair. Roads are crumbling, bridges are falling down, buildings are in need of repair, and playgrounds and schools are falling into disrepair. Streets are increasingly filthy. The elderly need care. Why can't welfare recipients perform some of these jobs? But there is a major obstacle to this proposal, and that is public employee unions. These unions see low-level public sector jobs like street cleaning and road maintenance as good-paying jobs for their members. Their most obvious fear is that low-paid welfare workers will be used to displace regular, highly paid union members. Even if no regular workers lose their jobs, and even if all workfare workers were paid the same as regular workers, workfare would still depress the wages of existing workers by forcing them to compete with people who, by definition, are low-paid. The public employee unions have been extremely successful in keeping welfare recipients from doing the street-cleaning and menial jobs that the larger society would like to see them doing.

In California, because of these unions no current state employees can be fired to make way for welfare workers, nor can any employee be deprived of overtime. No work customarily performed by union members may be performed by welfare recipients. And no jobs for welfare recipients may be opened at any agency in which regular employees are on layoff. These provisions make it impossible for welfare workers to work in state agencies. Their only hope is to be placed in private sector jobs, but these are sometimes hard to get. Work in the nonprofit sector, such as the United Way, the American Red Cross, the Urban League, and organizations that supply "adult services" and "child care services," is mentioned as a possibility for welfare workers. This nonprofit gambit sharply restricts the number of potential jobs. It also means that welfare workers will almost never actually build anything, clean anything, or perform any useful service that the government isn't already doing itself.

WHY WORK WORKS

African Americans everywhere should support welfare reform because even far-left writers like Cloward and Piven have to admit that "many recipients are black (although a bare majority are in fact white)."[17] As blacks make up only about 12 percent of the entire population in the United States, it is hardly comforting that Cloward and Piven note that a bare majority of recipients are white. I agree with Mickey Kaus, who argued in a previously cited article that "work works." The current reforms on the table are moving in the right direction. The expectation that women should work even if they have young children is good. I also believe that ghetto men ought to be given an opportunity to work in those public sector jobs, particularly if they are the fathers of babies whose mothers are on welfare.

Mickey Kaus's proposal, which was first suggested in the 1986 article discussed earlier, is a radical restructuring of welfare which is worthy of consideration. His plan would replace all cash-subsidy welfare programs that assist the able-bodied poor, such as AFDC, general relief, food stamps, and housing (but not Medicaid), with a single offer from the government of employment for every American citizen over eighteen who wants it, in a useful public job at a wage slightly below the minimum wage. If you could work and needed money, you would not be given a check (welfare). You would be given the location of several government job sites. If you showed up and worked, you would be paid for your work. If you didn't show up, you wouldn't get paid. Unlike "workfare" jobs, these jobs would be available to everybody, men as well as women, single or married, mothers and fathers alike. Anyone who showed up could work.

The major problem with the Kaus plan is the enormous cost of creating that many public sector jobs. Also, one could expect vigorous opposition from public sector employee unions. Kaus would keep the wage low so that only those most in need of work would show up for work and so that the incentive to look for better work in the private sector would be preserved. Yet this wage would not be enough to support a family and would be condemned by liberal critics who demand that welfare recipients receive wages high enough to lift their families beyond the poverty range. "We can't expect welfare recipients to flip hamburgers at $5.00 an hour," says Representative Harold E. Ford.[18] He wants wages to be $9.00 an hour. But there are ways to supplement the incomes of low-wage workers, particularly if there is free child care and some kind of transportation subsidy. The current earned-income tax credit could be expanded to increase the actual incomes of the welfare working poor. This tax credit also helps those already working who are poor. But most important for Kaus and others who agree with him, those who worked in these public jobs would be earning their money. They could hold their heads up. They would also have work experience and a work history and would be able to give the job as a reference when looking for a better job.

However, and this is the hard part for most liberals, those who didn't take advantage of these jobs would be on their own, including mothers who are able-bodied and able to work. Kaus's proposal would end all cash subsidies and punish those who refuse to work for their money. But what about today's reform proposals, which offer training and education? Would mothers be allowed to refuse to take advantage of them? At some point, someone will have to make the hard decision regarding cutting off recipients. For example, take the case of Yasmeen Nixon, a twenty-year-old single mother in her junior year of high school with one daughter. She was recently profiled in a 1994 *Businessweek* article and was quoted as saying she is not happy with the prospect of sending her daughter to a free child-care center. In fact, Nixon may decide to stay home with her daughter and suffer the sanctions of the law: "Why, just because I'm poor, should I have to take my kid down to some dark basement to play all day where all the dolls' heads are pulled off"? says Nixon.[19] Whether or not she is describing the majority of day care centers accurately, she shows that some people will not follow the program. One wonders what Nixon thinks about the millions of women who are not on welfare and who daily leave their children in day care centers (which may cost $50 to $60 per week) because they have to work. The point here is not Nixon's attitude, but whether administrators will have the courage to cut off recipients when they refuse to follow the rules.

The main goal of any welfare reform package must be to break the culture of poverty by providing jobs for ghetto men and women who may have had no prior work habits and at the same time by ending the option of a life on welfare for single mothers. The current attempts to reform the welfare system are trying to create a system in which status, dignity, and government benefits flow only to those who work, but in which the government steps in to make sure that work is available to all. Usually working does not come as second nature to those who have never worked. Some welfare mothers are going to have trouble with the new reforms. There will be cries of anguish and unhappiness at first because "the workplace is so foreign to so many people who are second- and third-generation dependents," says Tom Nees, a Washington, D.C., minister whose Community of Hope works with welfare families poor enough to be homeless.[20]

Since many of the welfare recipients will be taking public sector jobs, the question arises: Will there be enough of these jobs that people can do? Certainly if we look around our country there appear to be enough worthwhile jobs to

be done. The crumbling "infrastructure" that has been discussed over the years still hasn't been repaired. For financial
reasons, governments all around the country have stopped
doing things they once thought worthwhile, like opening
libraries on Saturday and picking up trash twice a week.
These would make good public sector jobs that would be
visible, so taxpayers could see their welfare dollars working
for them. But some are concerned about whether the welfare
recipients who would need public service jobs are capable of
doing all these worthwhile jobs. One objection has to do
with women and physical labor. Are we really going to have
teenage girls repairing potholes and painting bridges? One
response is: Why not? Says Mickey Kaus in response to this
question, "Women can fill potholes and paint bridges (and
water lawns and pick up garbage), just as women can be
telephone repairmen and sailors. Feminism has rightly destroyed the sex stereotypes that used to surround much
physical work. There are many nonarduous jobs that need
doing, such as nurses' aides, Xerox operators, receptionists,
clerks, coat checkers, cooks, and cleaners. Private schools
often require parents to keep order on playgrounds twice a
month. Public schools might employ one or two parents to
do the same full-time. Day-care centers could, too. Is there
any point in offering women free day care and then putting
some of them to work in day-care centers? Yes. First, that
would still free up a lot of women for employment. Second,
and more important, the day-care jobs would exist within
the culture of work—with alarm clocks to set, appointments
to keep, and bosses to please—rather than the culture of
welfare."[21]

    One objection to the current public-service jobs pro-
gram is that it will eventually degenerate into makework.
People who raise this objection cite the old CETA programs

of the late 1970s and early 1980s. CETA (Comprehensive Employment and Training Act) was a disaster for a variety of reasons, but one big reason was that doing anything useful would have offended the unions. Construction unions insisted on restrictions that basically precluded CETA from building anything or providing any useful service that might be performed by civil servants. So CETA workers were reduced to doing ridiculous kinds of jobs in experimental film workshops and mime troupes. In California they took a dog and cat census.

It is understandable that unions are opposed to public sector jobs. Undoubtedly these jobs will hurt them because the jobs will offer competition to union workers. However, if we are serious about breaking the poverty culture, we must be serious enough to sacrifice the interests of this protected group. Why should well-paid government workers be shielded from the competitive labor market at the expense of the poorest segment of society? Pragmatism, if not fairness, requires that no current government workers be laid off. As these workers leave through natural attrition, however, the government would be free to replace them with guaranteed jobholders. Guaranteed job projects could then be chosen on the basis of how useful they are, not whether a union objects to them. Wherever possible, they would be designed to produce a tangible benefit—collected garbage, a clean subway station, painted-over graffiti, a clean street— that the public could see.

The more jobs found in the private sector the better. These jobs would be gotten by developing close ties to local businesses that can provide jobs. Many of these jobs would probably require more skills than some of the public sector jobs. Also, these private sector jobs wouldn't pay much because they would be mainly entry-level. However, with child care and medical benefits, they would eventually lead to independence, or so it is hoped. The New Hope Project in Milwaukee, which began in 1990, is such a comprehensive program designed to get people into private sector jobs. It offers wage subsidy, child care, and health benefits, but only for parents who are working. Participants must look for private sector jobs, although they can work in community service jobs temporarily.[22]

In 1994, the economy was expanding and creating about 250,000 positions a month (as of July), which gives hope to welfare reformers because there is work. The only problem is that this work will probably offer only low pay. Many of the jobs are in the service industries, which traditionally offer low pay. And welfare recipients, who by definition are unemployed, would enter into these service jobs at the bottom of the salary ladder. Without child care, health care, and food stamps, these workers will not be able to leave the welfare rolls.

CONCLUSION

Unfortunately, I have not seen black Americans in the vanguard of welfare reform. In fact, most of the blacks I have heard on this issue have acted mainly as obstructionists to any meaningful changes in the welfare system. Only now that the system has grown so bad do we see some activity by black leaders, but this is mainly to protect the benefits of recipients. I find this unfortunate because these leaders are shortsighted. Welfare has not been a boon to blacks, but a bust. It is, as New Jersey lawmaker Wayne Bryant says, modern slavery. And while the debate rages on regarding whether welfare actually causes young black women to have babies out of wedlock, welfare enables these births. It provides a means of making the raising of these children, without fathers, possible. No one knows what price welfare recipients pay, in low self-esteem, for being on welfare. Welfare mothers, probably unfairly, are viewed as being on the bottom rung of the social ladder. Yet here they are raising children who will also probably have low self-esteem.

Even years ago, when I was growing up in South Central Los Angeles, black people had disdain for those on welfare, and if a person (usually a woman) had to collect it, she was always proud to say she no longer needed it. My mother worked as a domestic for years (she worked cleaning wealthy white families' homes) to supplement my father's income. I was proud of my mother's effort to keep us financially solvent and felt good about my family's status. My father, who only got to the fourth grade, drove a truck, and I saw him and my mother leave home every day for work. It didn't matter what kind of jobs they held. There was something dignified in what they did. My mother used to talk about how hard they had worked when they were sharecroppers in and around Waco, Texas. My story is not unique. Most black people came from the same hard-working families because years ago there was no relief or subsidy for anyone. I think we need to return to this same work tradition and impart that tradition to our children. Welfare does not give that sense of dignity to people. It was never meant to be a way of life, but a way out of hard times until things got better. It is now time to end welfare dependency and move back toward a work ethic.

CHAPTER SEVEN

The Declining Significance of Integration

Sam Donaldson, a reporter for ABC, seemed uncomfortable. He had been questioning several black civil rights leaders about race relations and integration in the aftermath of the 1992 Los Angeles riots, but they weren't giving him the answers he wanted to hear. Donaldson seemed particularly disturbed that some of the civil rights leaders no longer felt that their primary goal should be a racially integrated society. Indeed, many of these leaders placed racial integration low on their priority list. There is a real dichotomy of opinion in the black community. On the one hand, integration is no longer the primary goal of many blacks. On the other hand, there is this nagging historical belief that integration ought to be the goal. Some of the more traditional civil rights leaders lament the demise of integration as the primary goal of blacks. These black leaders are particularly concerned about the decline of school integration as a primary goal.

But school integration has been only marginally successful in recent years, and integration in other areas has lost some of its urgency. For example, in the area of housing, many (middle-class) blacks desire to live in neighborhoods that are safe and not rundown, but they are not particularly concerned about living next to whites. In fact, several communities are springing up all over America that boast of having exclusively black middle-class housing. These neighborhoods are segregated racially, but they could hardly be called ghettos.

Of course, integration in the workplace means jobs and earning a living. Black people are still quite adamant about employment opportunities, and rightfully so. Yet one of the most highly segregated institutions in America—namely, the churches—remains so. There has never been any great push to integrate churches. The fact is that both white and black people are happy to worship God in segregated facilities.

The May 1954 U.S. Supreme Court *Brown* ruling against school segregation was a landmark decision in the history of civil rights. However, forty some years later, school segregation still exists, primarily because of the mass movement of white citizens to the suburbs. And it appears that even the great movement to integrate schools has lost momentum. Black parents accept all-black schools, as long as these schools offer their children an adequate education. Black parents are no longer willing to accept busing as a mechanism for integrating schools because it is usually their kids who get bused. A 1993 study by the National School Boards Association reports that 66 percent of the nation's black children attend schools with mostly minority students. The separate black and white school systems that once kept children apart are no longer the problem. The *Brown* decision changed that. Today's trend stems from a decreasing number of white students, which many blame on white flight, especially from big-city schools. "We didn't have a crystal ball. Nobody could see what was coming, certainly not a huge demographic shift," says Constance Baker Morley, a federal judge in New York who worked with Thur-good Marshall at the Legal Defense and Educational Fund at the time of the *Brown* decision. "The cities were deterio-rating [and suburbs were being developed]. Even if the Supreme Court had never decided Brown, there was going to be white migration from the cities."[1] As white people fled urban areas with greater and greater speed, they took the tax base and their middle-class children with them to the suburbs.

Ironically, the southern states that once most strictly enforced legal segregation are today among those where black and white students are most integrated. According to the 1993 National School Boards Association (NSBA) study, the South still has the largest percentage of black students, but it is also the region that has the second largest percent-age (39 percent) attending predominantly white schools. The highest level of segregation currently exists in the Northeast, where no desegregation plan was thought neces-sary in 1954. There, only 24 percent of black students attend schools that are mostly white, while 50 percent attend schools that are 90 to 100 percent nonwhite. In the years immediately following the *Brown* decision, minority chil-dren made up a little more than one-eighth of our elemen-tary through high school population; now they constitute approximately one-third. Interestingly, the greatest segrega-tion of students no longer involves black children. The most segregated group in the nation's public schools today is the rapidly increasing population of Hispanic students.[2]

In 1989 the NSBA observed in its report, "The United States [has] a shrinking proportion of white students and a rising share of black and Hispanic students who experience far less success than whites in American public education and are concentrated in schools with lower achievement levels and less demanding competition. These trends suggest the Supreme Court's 1954 conclusion that intentionally segregated schools are 'inherently unequal' remains true today."[3]

But are blacks still dedicated to integrated schools? The answer to that question lies in a recent development that occurred in one of the schools in Oklahoma City. In a 1991 article "Separate and Equal," James Traub discusses the case of Northeast High School, which had been a segregated school in 1961. In fact, says Traub, the Oklahoma City School Board had been sued by a black parent for refusing to allow his son admission to the school. Yet years later, after the school had been forced to integrate, the world had again turned upside down. Now the same school board proposed a return to the status quo of 1961. A committee of the school board, led by a black man, was proposing a return to neighborhood schools at the elementary-school level.[4]

An interesting thing about the Northeast High School development was that the great majority of parents spoke in favor of the new plan, even though it would return many of their children to segregated elementary schools (an option of the plan allowed black parents to send their children to a white-majority school, using transportation provided by the school board). Civil rights activists bitterly reproached the board members for marching backward. But the activists constituted a distinct minority, and they were seen as remnants of an older order. "It was very painful," says Susan Hermes, who chaired the school board at the time and is an advocate of the plan. "Many of these people have fought for civil rights all their lives. The most difficult part for them is to let go of that and let people work together in other ways."[5]

The NAACP Legal Defense Fund took the school board

to court, as it had years earlier. After five years the matter landed in the U.S. Supreme Court. The case was expected to provide the most important busing decision of recent years. In mid-January 1991, the Court concluded that a school board can be released from court-ordered busing and can even permit some resegregation as long as it has taken all "practicable" steps to eliminate the "vestiges" of past discrimination. The case was remanded to federal court, where it remains.

While many civil rights activists were terribly unhappy with the results of this Oklahoma City case, most of the parents and teachers and administrators viewed the neighborhood plan for elementary schools in nonracial terms. These black parents seemed to reiterate what school integration was all about, namely, a good education for their kids and not integration for integration's sake. Many of the Oklahoma parents stated they believed in integration but were more concerned about the quality of their children's education. And they believed that their children could get an equal education in a racially separate setting, which appeared to be a historic change for black America from the old civil rights days. Is this really a historic change? Actually many blacks, including U.S. Supreme Court Justice Clarence Thomas, disagreed with the 1954 *Brown* school desegregation decision. The disagreement was not with the result, ending separate-but-equal, but with how the case was argued. Much of the Supreme Court's reasoning had come from research conducted by Kenneth Clark and published in his book *Dark Ghetto* (1965). Using Clark's discussion about lower self-esteem among black children who are raised in segregated situations, the Court stated that segregated schools were inherently unequal and caused harm to black children. This argument, when taken to its logical conclusions, seemed to suggest that blacks could not develop normal, healthy self-esteem without the presence of whites. Clarence Thomas objected to the decision's conclusions, not to the results (he was viciously attacked for his objection, even though he tried to explain that he was not against integrated schools). Thomas's objection has some merit because the *Brown* decision flies in the face of the tradition of black colleges in America. No one would suggest that these institutions be dismantled because they have all-black student bodies.

THE CASE FOR BLACK SCHOOLS

Many Americans, both black and white, support black colleges. Yet the idea of having all-black-male schools created a tremendous amount of controversy when it was proposed by black educators in 1991. The rationale for all-male black schools was the argument that black males were not succeeding in traditional school settings. Those who proposed these black schools believed that black males—many of whom came from female-dominated families—would benefit from an environment which was black-male-dominated. These black male teachers would serve as both role models and mentors to these black male youths and would hopefully intervene in their negative lifestyles.

One of the first cities to take up the debate was New York City, and in mid-January 1991 the New York City Board of Education sympathetically discussed a proposal for an all-black, "African-centered" high school. In another article, written in 1991, and called "Ghetto Blasters: The Case for All-Black Schools," James Traub says, "The proposal was throttled by fierce opposition but appears to have been revived by an endorsement from Mayor David Dinkins. The Detroit school board recently backed a plan for a similar school. One elementary school in Baltimore established an all-black-male class last year [1990]. This September [1991] the Milwaukee public schools will open the doors on two 'African-American Immersion Schools,' at the elementary and junior high school levels."[6]

The prospect of racially segregated schools provoked horror among civil rights leaders. The National Organization for Women opposed the schools because they were mainly for black males and not females. The counterargument to that objection was that black females are not at the same risk as black males. After all, our prisons are filled with black males, not black females. The American Civil Liberties Union spoke about these schools as being in violation of Title VI of the 1964 Civil Rights Act. The NAACP and other civil rights groups also voiced their opposition to these all-male black schools. But what if all-black schools prove to have some educational value for children who otherwise seem doomed to failure? All-black schools, like other educational novelties, can be well or poorly designed. Right now the fixation on an "Afrocentric" curriculum means that the proposed schools are likely to be mired in dubious pedagogy. But that needn't be the case. A school that seriously tries to address the problems of underclass children is worth trying.

Yet the critics of these schools seem to miss the point. In reality we already have mostly all-black schools in our cities. Whites have long since departed to the suburbs, making real integration impossible unless we are willing to undertake massive busing. There is no political will in this country to return to massive busing. White people didn't like busing because it brought about the very thing they were trying to escape, which was having their kids go to urban schools. Black people didn't like busing because, as was said earlier, it was their kids who got bused.

In reality we have segregated schools anyway. Detroit's school system is 90 percent black. Proponents of all-black schools say anger at "resegregation" is a moot point. "A lot of people who talk about this don't understand the reality we're dealing with," says Norman Fruchter, a grants officer at the Aaron Diamond Foundation, which has offered to underwrite the New York school. "In a lot of the public schools in New York City de facto segregation is the rule."[7]

But when schools desegregate, how successful are black students? Milwaukee's is a good example of an integrated school system. It has lived under a court order since 1977, and though the system population is almost 60 percent black, all but 19 of its 150 schools are deemed integrated.[8] But integration has not always had the equalizing effect that was expected from the demise of separate-but-equal. A task force appointed in 1991 found that in the city's 15 high schools, all but 1 integrated, white students averaged a score of about 60 on a reading test administered in the tenth grade, and blacks about 25. Black students also lagged behind whites in math. The task force took the findings as an indictment of the schools and recommended to the school board an ambitious all-black school experiment.[9]

Part of the impetus for all-black-male schools is the disenchantment with integration. But I believe there is another larger issue at stake. I think that the black community, and in particular its middle class, no longer feels it needs to integrate. Except for remnants of the old civil rights establishment, there is no push from the black community to integrate into white America. Of course, there are financial considerations, but I think that for the first time a significant segment of the black community no longer feels the need to be integrated with whites. Integration is a benevolent idea, but in America it usually meant blacks' going into white schools or neighborhoods. It certainly didn't mean whites integrating with blacks, except as professionals such as social workers, police, or firefighters. Blacks, I believe, held onto the idea of integration because they needed validation from the white world. But today that need, as I call it, is fading and will eventually allow real integration to occur, though it might take many years. I think overall it is a healthy development for the black community.

Anyway, the proponents of all-black-male segregated schools say, "We're just saying that we have to try something to see if we can't improve the academic performance of black boys," says Joyce Mallory, head of the Milwaukee School Board.[10] Black children, especially black boys, suffer disproportionately from the debilitating effects of poverty, violence, and splintered families. Boys with no father at home—two-thirds of the black male students in Milwaukee, says Ken Holt, a high school principal who is directing the development of the new schools—are not likely to relate well to school authority.[11]

The proposed all-black-male schools tend to stress values and a sense of community. Teachers are expected to make extraordinary commitments to students. Milwaukee is planning to have teachers stay with the same students for several years. In the school proposed for Detroit, students will be expected to wear a jacket and tie to class. The proponents of all-black-male schools cite the success of inner-city parochial schools, many of which are virtually all-black, as examples of how all-male black schools can work. There is solid evidence that parochial schools, with their clear sense of purpose and their emphasis on discipline and academic rigor, do better with poor minority children than do public schools. Catholic schools in inner cities have been available to the mainly black and Hispanic middle or working middle classes. In South Central Los Angeles, the Holy Name Catholic School is entirely black and Hispanic.

What frightens many away from these schools is not their ethnic makeup, but their curriculum. Says Traub, "But then there's the Afrocentric part. Advocates simply take it for granted that a curriculum that stresses the achievements and history of black Americans and Africans will bolster the self-esteem of black students by giving them positive role models. . . . The idea that black—and white—students need to learn more about black culture and history is hardly controversial. However, the goal of the Afrocentrists is not to supplement the content of school curriculum, but to transform it."[12] The opponents of these schools believe that the real problem with them is not the fact of racial isolation, which is already a reality, but the divisiveness of the Afrocentrism that these schools seem likely to practice. Yet there are examples of the concept of an all-black-male structure working. An experiment in Dade County involving two all-black-male classes at the kindergarten and first-grade levels drastically reduced disciplinary problems and increased academic performance by having a strong principal and stressing a return to basics.[13] While schools cannot be expected to act as surrogates for stable families and communities, they can make a difference. By focusing on the problems of poor inner-city children in an all-black, or even an all-black-male, setting, schools may be able to create an atmosphere in which students can concentrate and even learn.

BLACK CONSERVATISM OR NATIONALISM
AND INTEGRATION

Many blame the resurgence of black nationalism for the demise of integration as a major goal of American blacks. But what many don't know is that there is a nexus between nationalism and what is called black conservatism. The roots of black nationalism can be found in today's black conservatism. Contrary to popular belief, black nationalism is a politically right, not liberal, movement. It is opposite to integrationist thinkers who believe we can all live together in harmony. Nationalists are more likely to support all-black institutions and to favor black self-help. Groups like the Nation of Islam are black nationalist in nature. Black nationalists supported Marcus Garvey, who led a back-to-Africa movement during the 1920s. Malcolm X was a black nationalist, and a strong admirer of Malcolm X and black nationalism is Clarence Thomas, U.S. Supreme Court Justice. During a 1987 interview with black *Washington Post* reporter Juan Williams (Williams is also the author of the award-winning book *Eyes on the Prize*, which is a history of the civil rights movement in America), Thomas was able to quote these words of Malcolm X from memory: "The American black man should be focusing his every effort toward building his own businesses and decent homes for himself. As other ethnic groups have done, let the black people, wherever possible, patronize their own kind, hire their own kind, and start in those ways to build up the black race's ability to do for itself. That's the only way the American black man is ever going to get respect."[14] The Malcolm X that Thomas invoked was a Black Power version of Horatio Alger. "I don't see how the civil rights people today can claim Malcolm X as one of their own," Thomas told Williams. "Nor does he say black people should go begging to the Labor Department for jobs. He was hell on integrationists. Where does he say you should sacrifice your institutions to be next to white people?"[15]

Thomas is a classic black conservative-nationalist. The key to what he stands for is best located in his own frequent references to natural law, the Declaration of Independence, Abraham Lincoln, and the first great black Republican, Frederick Douglass. In Clarence Thomas's emphasis on natural law and the principles of the Declaration, he, too, insists that America stands for a moral project that includes blacks as much as whites. He insists that the morality of individualism that underlies the U.S. Constitution applies to all and provides opportunities for all. But he also asserts that full inclusion requires efforts that may be at odds with the ethos of affirmative action and the implicit teaching of many welfare-state programs. In his opposition to affirmative action, Thomas avoids the mistaken argument, made by many conservatives, that affirmative action is simply discrimination in reverse (as if affirmative action were based on the idea that whites are inferior or second-class citizens). Instead, he argues that affirmative action undermines the moral resources that blacks need in order to earn their way into the American mainstream. Thomas's concern is that group-based preferences encourage blacks to look to government largess rather than to self-help and individual initiative.

Indeed, for Thomas, as well as for many other prominent black conservatives like Walter Williams, who is an economics professor at George Mason University, integration itself has been a mixed blessing. They suggest that it helped put many black enterprises out of business and thus undermined the initiative and self-reliance of black communities. And they believe that much recent social policy has been more of a burden than a benefit. Welfare teaches dependency, and busing assumes that all-black schools necessarily suffer without the presence of white students. (See Juan Williams, 1987.) Black conservatives or nationalists argue that all of these policies and programs meant to bring about racial parity represent losses as well as gains. They fear that a principle of dependency is nurtured in these programs designed to help blacks: a teaching that blacks are incapable of doing for themselves. Thomas and Williams are not the only black conservatives who are concerned.

Other black conservatives, such as Glenn Loury, Shelby Steele, and Thomas Sowell, also worry that these welfare programs have blacks assuming the role of victimhood. These programs brought the rise of a civil rights lobby whose livelihood depends on spawning programs and fostering a taste for them. Thomas articulated this position well in a commencement address he made at Savannah State College in 1985. He warned of "wallowing in excuses," and of "being lured by sirens and purveyors of misery who profit from constantly regurgitating all that is wrong with black Americans and blaming these problems on others."[16] The core of Thomas's argument is its insistence on the reality and the redemptive potential of black pride. "Past generations of blacks," he said at Savannah, "knew all too well that they were held back by prejudice. But they weren't pinned down by it."[17] This emphasis on the necessity of self-help and the denial of a government route to dignity helps explain Thomas's, as well as other black conservatives', sympathy with aspects of Malcolm X and Louis Farrakhan (these conservatives tend to eschew Farrakhan's anti-Semitism): Blacks have been victimized, but at base they are not victims. Thomas's argument against affirmative action and the governmental path to equality is based on the judgment that equal standing as a citizen comes from individual effort; that dignity and pride of citizenship in America cannot be conferred by affirmative or any government action; that all immigrant groups—from Irish Catholics, to Jews, to Asians—have suffered discrimination and progressed by dint of their own effort (as Thomas Sowell has long argued). In this regard, Thomas belongs to a long tradition of conservative thinking about the role of government in America. The government should enforce the rules of fair play and then leave individuals to succeed or not on their own.

In terms of race relations, the conservative view believes that government should enforce desegregation, not necessarily force integration. Historically, segregation was enforced by state laws which were oppressive. However, integration connotes a voluntary component. Institutions of higher learning are desegregated in America, but hardly socially integrated. As was stated earlier, churches remain racially apart, but one would hesitate to use the word *segregated*. Nor is there a push for desegregating America's churches. Black nationalism and conservatism come to a nexus on many issues regarding race. How important is a racially integrated society? Can white and black people be ultimately happy in a racially separate America? While many black leaders publicly deplore the demise of integration as a goal, they privately push a different agenda. Why? Because of the increasing conservatism among black Americans.

A poll conducted in 1992 by the Joint Center for Political and Economic Studies, a liberal black think tank, found that while 72 percent of black Americans identified themselves as Democrats (and only 5 percent as Republicans), they did not identify themselves as liberals. In fact, more blacks characterized themselves as conservative (33 percent) than liberal (29 percent). And this was no maverick poll. A series of *Washington Post* polls conducted in 1991 found that blacks rarely classified themselves as "conservative Republicans." Among 445 blacks surveyed, only 8 percent described themselves this way. When the term *Republican* was taken out of the question, however, 35 percent identified themselves as "conservative" or "very conservative."[18] Over the years, surveys of politically contentious issues have consistently corroborated this incongruity. Nearly 60 percent of blacks favor the death penalty and 85 percent support school choice, according to recent Gallup polls.[19] Of the black public, 53 percent disapprove of mandatory busing, and 77 percent feel that minorities should not receive preferential treatment to make up for past discrimination. According to survey data, "black people have more in common with Jerry Falwell than [with] Jesse Jackson," says Walter Williams, one of the luminaries of the black conservative movement.[20] But even though blacks register conservative attitudes across the board, they will still say they're not Republican or conservative. There's a stigma that's associated with these labels in the black community.[21]

As the black community has become more conservative in nature, so has it moved away from liberal notions about an integrated society. Black colleges and universities have enjoyed a resurgence of popularity among prospective black students. All-black schools for males, which were discussed earlier, were something unheard of during the turbulent civil rights era but are now a serious policy proposal suggested by black educators. Even today's black political leaders like Jesse Jackson, says Danny Bakewell, Sr., a private developer who heads the Brotherhood Crusade Black United Fund (one of the most influential black organizations in Los Angeles), are privately moving toward self-help, community development, and the nurturing of an independent black entrepreneurial economy. Bakewell (who is a good friend of Jackson's) says that, in public speeches, Jackson and other leaders emphasize such programs as affirmative action and special treatment for minority-owned businesses, but behind the scenes, the traditional civil rights community also recognizes the importance of entrepreneurship, "and when we talk in private among ourselves, we talk about self-help and entrepreneurship," says Bakewell, whose organization sponsors seminars on starting businesses. "What we actually think is not what you hear in the speeches. There's a new consciousness in the community today."[22]

Self-help and entrepreneurship, not integration, are the main agenda for black nationalists. Understandably, those who are the most conservative have the least to gain from integration. It is not surprising that the poorest Americans in the inner cities register the most conservative social and economic values, according to recent polls, while the black middle class, many of whom are college-educated, tend to hold values that are more liberal and integrationist.

I agree with Danny Bakewell and others who say the black community is becoming more conservative. I would also suggest that with this new conservatism will come varying kinds of self-help efforts. For example, in Philadelphia, a grandfather, Herman Wrice, started a small, neighborhood organization to fight drug crime, and it has spread to 300 other neighborhoods throughout the country.[23] In Washington, retired police officer W. W. Johnson has brought thirty young boys into his home, where he inculcates conservative moral and social values.[24] In Los Angeles, Leon Watkins sits by the phone at the Family Help Line, which he founded, offering conservative advice and solutions to South Central families in need. Jesse Peterson prefers personal contact, roaming the streets and shelters of downtown Los Angeles disseminating a conservative social message to wayward black men.[25] "There are rumblings in the black community that most outsiders cannot see or feel," says Emanuel McLittle, publisher of the black conservative magazine *Destiny: The New Black American Mainstream.* "While white viewers listen to Jesse Jackson rant on TV, black people are sitting in front of their own TVs saying, 'This guy's got to be kidding!'"[26]

Empirical data reinforce the existence of a growing black conservatism at grass-roots levels. A Northwestern University study of the Chicago metropolitan area that compared black attitudes in 1990 with those in 1991 discerned a subtle shift to the right among individuals who identified themselves as being moderately liberal, moderately conservative, or middle of the road. And a recent *Washington Post* poll discovered large statistical gaps between the political attitudes of liberal black leaders and those of the black public they claim to represent. Some attribute inner-city conservatism to the black church, which has served as a social and moral center for poor blacks since slavery. In fact, contrary to popular television and rap video images of black America, studies show that poor blacks are among the most religious ethnic groups in America. "If you want to see what black people are all about, all you have to do is get up on a Sunday morning and stand in front of the churches," says Starr Parker, publisher of *NFTA,* or *Not Forsaking the Assembly,* a black Christian magazine. "That's what black people are doing. They're not rappin'. They're not stealing. They're praying."[27] Others attribute the conservatism to general frustration and disillusionment with liberal antipoverty programs that have proved unsuccessful. "The liberal Democrats have been the ones who have delivered the fish for all these years," says Representative Franks. "Prior to the welfare system that was established in the 1940s, not only did we survive, we were a lot better off. People didn't starve to death. But now we've produced generation after generation of welfare-dependent individuals."[28]

Still others say that black conservatism is a direct response to widespread disillusionment with traditional black leadership as represented by civil rights organizations such as the National Association for the Advancement of Colored People, the Urban League, the Southern Christian Leadership Conference, and the Congress of Racial Equality. Such groups are criticized for repeatedly demanding legal equality as a solution to the social ills within black America, without recognizing that many of the ills are immune to legal remedies. "The NAACP is still talking about Selma, Ala., and freedom rides, and that's no longer relevant to today's problems," says Kevin Pritchett. "It was good for back then, but right now we need to figure out how to get people jobs."[29]

This debate is nothing new. At the turn of the century, former slave Booker T. Washington and Harvard-educated historian W. E. B. DuBois went head to head on legal versus economic solutions to "the Negro problem." Washington established the Tuskegee Institute, an industrial school for blacks in Alabama, to preach his philosophy of technological specialization, hard work, and industry. Only economic self-sufficiency, said Washington, would propel blacks into mainstream American society. At the time, Washington was branded an Uncle Tom by DuBois, who helped found the NAACP in 1910. DuBois demanded full social equality for blacks and chastised Washington for condemning the black race to perpetual inferiority and manual labor. The NAACP and later the other black civil rights organizations took up the DuBois vision, demanding full legal equality first, and assuming that economic development would follow. Such was not to be the case, however. Economic improvement in black communities did not follow in the wake of the legal equality established in the mid-1960s with the Civil Rights and Voting Rights acts. While the end to legal discrimination provided an opportunity for many blacks, others were left behind.

During the late 1960s and early 1970s, American cities saw the rise of some of the worst social dysfunction among poor blacks in American history; hence the rise of the inner city. "Poor black people are simply fed up," says Joe Brown of the *Press Citizen*. "Many are old enough to remember a time when things just weren't like this. Even when racism was in its heyday you didn't have the mess you have now. And you can't blame it on Reagan or lack of government programs. People are starting to realize the simple fact that we've gotten away from the traditional values that sustained us through the worst of times—through slavery and lynchings and Jim Crow. And they're starting to do something about it."[30]

Many of the new grass-roots conservatives are Democrats; some even call themselves liberals—old-style liberals in the style of Martin Luther King, Jr., and Roy Wilkins, who talked about civil rights for everyone and equality of opportunity along with personal responsibility and moral superiority. What is most noteworthy about these individuals is not what they're for, but what they're against. They share a disgust for mainstream black rhetoric that ascribes the myriad social ailments within inner cities to racism and structural poverty rather than to personal behavior. They espouse a back-to-basics approach with an emphasis on self-help and neighborhood activism. "The vast majority of our community is indeed law abiding," says Ezola Foster, founder of Black Americans for Family Values, based in Los Angeles. "We feel that corrupt politicians and snake oil preachers are misleading our community. They keep the flames of racism burning rather than focusing on positive things. . . . We have to start by telling our children the truth. Number one, they're not African-Americans, they're Americans. Number two, our justice system may not be perfect, but it's the best one in the world. Number three, public school education is free; go to it and get it. It may not be the best deal, but they can get enough to succeed. Number four, work hard and rely on good character. It's such a simple message—but none of our black leaders are saying it!"[31]

Joe Clark, a former principal of Eastside High School in Paterson, New Jersey, says, "Black Americans have been betrayed by the condescending Jesse Jacksons who are not really concerned about the ultimate incorporation of blacks into the democratic process, but are more concerned with keeping them alienated and poor so that they can remain in power." Clark's tough-guy disciplinarian tactics won him his students' respect, the school board's wrath, and Hollywood's attention. (The movie *Lean on Me* was based on his story.) "Our inner-city youth lack discipline. Our kids are out of control. And racism and being poor has nothing to do with it," Clark says. "There was more racism and poverty when I was a kid. But we didn't pull this kind of outlandish crap, because there was a structure that did not permit that. We had families with strong morals and religion. We didn't have rampant promiscuity, illegitimacy and drug dependence. That's the result of liberalism and its anything-goes mentality."[32]

Many feel that classical liberalism, with its emphasis on social justice and equality, is not to blame; what is to blame is how liberalism has evolved in American politics, to include race-conscious policies such as affirmative action, preferential quotas, and race norming, as well as Afrocentrism and political correctness, which they say encourage animosity toward whites and self-segregation of blacks. The dismal state of black inner cities, saturated with crime, drugs, promiscuity, and hopelessness, they say, is testimony to the failure of the expansive antipoverty programs of the 1960s and 1970s. They believe that those programs destroyed the work ethic of many blacks, fostered greater dependencies, and led to the new cult of revolutionary blackness—exemplified by rap videos and "X" caps, common in inner cities, which signify allegiance to black separatist Malcolm X—which condones anger without providing an agenda for progress.

Because conservatives, black and white alike, are constantly criticizing the existing black structure—leadership, rhetoric, and popular culture—they are often portrayed in the media as negativists who condemn the existing system but offer nothing new in its stead. Black conservatives' issues—such as free-enterprise zones, tenant management of public housing, a youth subminimum wage, school vouchers, mandatory workfare, and increasing the savings cap for those on public aid—are rarely discussed in the mainstream press as part of an alternative package that black conservatives are offering. Part of the problem is that there has never been a popular forum through which they can publicize their ideas. Until now. *Destiny* is one of a handful of relatively conservative journals struggling to spread the word. In New York, Elizabeth Wright edits a quarterly journal, *Issues and Views*, as an "open forum on issues affecting the black community." In Los Angeles, Starr Parker has spearheaded NFTA's effort to spread the black conservative gospel. In Houston, Willie and Gwen Daye Richardson's *National Minority Politics* has just hit the newsstands. "We wanted to refute the idea that there are only five black conservatives in the entire country—the ones they always drag out," says Gwen Daye Richardson, referring to black conservative godfathers Thomas Sowell, Walter Williams, Glenn Loury, Robert Woodson, and Anne Wortham. "That's only the tip of the iceberg. We're all over the place. I'd say a third of the black community disagrees with the liberal position, and there could be more if the media would show more than one side."[33]

Even the radio waves are buzzing with the incantations of a small but vocal group of black conservatives, such as Ron Edwards in Detroit and Armstrong Williams in Washington. Williams, a former press secretary for Clarence Thomas during his years at the Equal Employment Opportunity Commission, decided to speak out after he saw how the media described black conservatism during coverage of the Anita Hill–Thomas hearings. "What the media has [sic] led blacks in this country to believe is that if you're a white liberal, you can't be racist, but if you're a white or a black Republican, you can," says Williams. "For anybody to believe that is just dumb."[34] Williams points out that Clinton received 88 percent of the black vote, even though as governor of Arkansas he didn't support a civil rights bill in his state. "That would have been a campaign-altering issue if Clinton had been a Republican," he says, reminding listeners that George Bush appointed more blacks to his administration than any other American president. Keith Butler, a black Republican council member in Detroit, also complains about a double standard: "If a Republican is saying welfare reform, blacks tend to think they want to dump them off; they hate us. But if Bill Clinton says welfare reform, they say 'Okay, he wants to get the dead-beats off.' "[35]

Black conservatives are continually frustrated not only by the black public's ignorance of Republican principles, but also by the Republican Party's seeming lack of interest in rectifying its image among blacks. Bill Calhoun, a Houston entrepreneur and chair of the Black Republican Council of Texas, chastises the party for not taking advantage of the conservative winds blowing in black America. Republicans, he says, have conceded the black vote because they get so little of it, but if they would listen closely to what's being said rather than to past exit polls, they might see a productive source of new votes: "The party has written off the black vote, and as a result there's much indifference toward looking at new ways to get the message out. There has to be a new effort to overcome black suspicion and let African-Americans in on what conservative Republicanism is all about."[36] Gwen Daye Richardson agrees: "The Republicans are missing it. They're not coming into the community to find out the real heartbeat of inner-city blacks. They're sitting in Washington listening to pollsters instead of listening to what people are really saying out here."[37]

Some conservatives worry not only that the Republican Party is losing its chance to tap into black grass-roots conservatism, but also that liberals may be using this conservatism to their own advantage. They see liberal leaders subtly changing their discourse to include phrases such as "personal responsibility." "If you listen to Jesse Jackson's speeches today, they have much more of a self-reliance approach," says Lee Walker, president of the New Coalition for Economic and Social Change, a new black conservative think tank in Chicago. "The Urban League is now using the term 'self-help.' I don't think you would have heard these phrases used 10 years ago. The liberal intellects and politicians have discovered that if they don't get involved in this debate with respect to black conservatism, they're going to be out of the discussion altogether."[38] Even black activist Al Sharpton is beginning to change his tune, urging black high school students to stay in school and away from guns. It's time to "bring down the volume and bring up the program," he told an interviewer in January. The late Republican strategist Lee Atwater often argued that the GOP could become the majority party if only it could persuade a mere 10 percent of black Americans to switch affiliation and return to the party of Lincoln. Today the consensus seems to be that if any Republican has the ability to "steal" a substantial portion of the black vote from the Democrats, it's former Housing and Urban Development Secretary Jack Kemp, whose strategies for empowering poor Americans appeal to black conservative instincts. "The only person who can overcome the stigma is someone like Kemp," says council member Butler of Detroit. "Someone who is loved by both blacks and whites, liberals and conservatives, who has the ability to cross over. You need someone who is able to communicate the message that people can rally behind and get around preconceived ideas and stereotypes."[39]

Leon Watkins of L.A.'s Family Help Line couldn't agree more. He says "black folks" in South Central are starting to vote more for individual candidates than in lockstep with the party. If Kemp runs in 1996, Watkins says, he'll get on the phone with a "whole network" of other grass-roots leaders, and they'll get out the black vote. "Both parties had better pay attention in '96," he warns, "or they're going to miss out. We're voting for the person, not the party. We're voting for issues, not ideology." In this case, the Republican Party and its Kempian conservative ideology may wind up being the chief beneficiaries. Jesse Peterson says that many of the problems that seem endemic to black inner cities can be traced to the failure of the black man and the dissolution of traditional family structure. He knows, he says, from personal experience. Until he was thirty-seven, says Peterson, he, too, was brainwashed by traditional black rhetoric into thinking all his problems were due to "the white man." Now forty-three and the owner of a successful janitorial business, Peterson says he has seen the light, and he's spreading it to young men throughout South Central Los Angeles through BOND, or Brotherhood Organization of a New Destiny, which he founded. Peterson makes regular visits to schools, homeless shelters, halfway houses, and bus stop benches—anyplace he thinks he'll find young black men in need of direction. "Our purpose," he says, "is to rebuild the black community by rebuilding the black man. The black community is a mess, not because of white people, but because the man himself is weak. He is overcome by hate, which has taken over his life. There's no sense of self-reliance, self-control, principles or character."[40]

Peterson disputes those who attribute the ills of black neighborhoods to unemployment. "The reason that the unemployment rate is so high in the black community is because we have not provided job opportunities for ourselves," he says. "We believe the lie that comes from black politicians and liberals that the white man owes us a job. As a result, it kept us from creating jobs in our own community. We are our worst enemies, and we're always blaming others."[41] Not everyone likes Peterson's message. He says he is called an Uncle Tom and has received threatening calls. He was even fired as host of a radio talk show for views described as confrontational, insensitive, and sexist. But Peterson remains unrepentant. "Our leaders have only led us astray," he says, referring to Jesse Jackson, California Representative Maxine Waters, former Los Angeles Mayor Tom Bradley, and the Reverend Cecil Murray of South Central's First African Methodist Episcopal Church. "They lied and kept us angry by reminding us that we couldn't make it because of slavery; by blaming our problems on white America; by using racism as an excuse for irresponsible behavior. They don't lead; they just spread hate."[42] Who would Peterson prefer to provide leadership for black Americans? He speaks glowingly of black conservatives such as Thomas Sowell, Walter Williams, and Glenn Loury. "They are perfect examples of what we should all strive to be," he says. "They are self-reliant, independent thinkers who stand for something." The problem, says Peterson, is that few inner-city blacks have heard of them: "When I first began to overcome, I wasn't aware of black conservative thinkers because the media had not shown us any. Conservatism was something I came to without knowing it. I just knew I had to change my life."[43]

Nine years ago, Starr Parker was a single mother on welfare. Today she publishes a conservative Christian magazine in Los Angeles that is expected to gross more than $200,000 this year. Parker decided to start the magazine to provide a forum for the "other" voices of black America and to "let America at large know that there is another side to this story; that most blacks are not in step with what you would hear most of the civil rights organizations say today." Reaching more than 30,000 readers in the metropolitan area, *NFTA*, or *Not Forsaking the Assembly*, takes tough stands on everything from welfare dependency to homosexuals in the military. "Everybody knows welfare is wrong," says Parker.

"No one wants to live on the county. Black folks are like everyone else. They want to be able to provide for their own families and be able to be given the opportunities that are available throughout our society to propel themselves. Nobody wants to be given handouts and have people think for them. But if someone's going to give you $400 a month, plus a couple of hundred dollars of food stamps, free child care, education, and health care, and let you do whatever you want to do in the meantime, wouldn't you take it? We know it, and they know it," she says, referring to the "liberal establishment" that generated the social welfare programs. "But welfare is a billion-dollar industry. If they solve the poverty problem, a lot of folks would be unemployed."[44] Black enterprise and business, says Parker, are the only way to heal the social and economic infirmity within black inner cities such as Inglewood, California, where she lives. This young entrepreneur calculates that she received about $25,000 over the years she collected Aid to Families with Dependent Children (AFDC). "If they had given me that in one check," she muses, "man, my business would be twice what it is today."[45]

On any given night, in West Philadelphia, Herman Wrice is waging what may be the most effective anticrime battle American inner cities have seen in a long time. Wrice formed Mantua against Drugs six years ago out of a sense of frustration with liberal drug and crime-prevention policies and a feeling of personal impotence. Since then he has become a self-proclaimed conservative, and his grass-roots organization has spread to 300 neighborhoods across the country. His methods are simple: Hang out on street corners and force drug dealers to find other, more subdued areas for their trade. If enough neighborhoods are taken back, the dealers will have no place to go. "We tried everything we could to eliminate the drug sales by using the normal liberal approach—speaking with the Police Department and the City Council and blaming welfare and the schools," Wrice says. "And then it dawned on us that the problem was our own inability to get up off our fat butts and go do something about it. So we started to take our neighborhoods back, and then the rest of the conservative approach just kind of followed. We didn't start off trying to be conservatives; we started off trying to solve a drug problem and found out you can't do it liberally. It just so happens that common sense is called conservative."[46]

White liberals, says Wrice, have been unable to produce the results for inner cities that two decades of study groups, conferences, and a diffusion of programs promised. Today, according to *Time* magazine, as many as 135,000 American students bring guns into school every day, primarily because of drugs. In 1986, an average of one child a day was shot in Detroit. And nationwide, blacks are 60 percent more likely than whites to be victims of violent crimes. "People are saying something's wrong—something's wrong with expecting the government to solve our problems for us," says Wrice. "We've got to start doing something ourselves about it."[47] Wrice is equally disgusted by liberal black leaders who blame inner-city dysfunction on white racism. Becoming conservative, he says, "is just something that happens when black people get pushed around enough and realize that we're getting pushed around by people who have the same color faces that we've got."[48]

BLACK INDEPENDENCE

In 1934, the brilliant black thinker W. E. B. DuBois was dismissed from the editorship of the NAACP's magazine

Crisis because of his view that the drive for integration at all costs undermined black people's confidence in their won institutions and capabilities. Fearing that the fight against segregation had become a crusade to mix with whites for its own sake, DuBois wrote, "Never in the world should our fight be against association with ourselves because by that token we give up the whole argument that we are worth associating with."[49] But as was mentioned earlier, Kenneth Clark succeeded in convincing the U.S. Supreme Court that segregation was inherently damaging to the personalities of black children. Unless whites were willing to mix with blacks, then black children would suffer. This intellectual perspective seemed to say that blacks could have no self-respect that was not validated by whites. Of this perspective, civil rights veteran Floyd McKissick once noted sarcastically, "If you put Negro with Negro you get stupidity."[50] Such expressions of black insecurity and inferiority were inevitable in light of the direction the civil rights movement seemed to take in school integration.

Black neoconservatism is a backlash, in some sense, against the traditional civil rights approach. It is ruggedly independent and self-reliant. This new approach, which really isn't new at all, is an attempt to move blacks away from dependence on either welfare or white institutions and to create a more independent black community.

CHAPTER EIGHT

Black Empowerment

A HISTORY OF BLACK SELF-HELP
AND ENTREPRENEURSHIP IN AMERICA

In 1909, about fifty years before the modern civil rights movement emerged, the National Association for the Advancement of Colored People (NAACP) was founded following the lynching of a black man in Springfield, Illinois. Its first major undertaking was the fight against the hundreds of such atrocities then occurring annually. The Urban League was founded the next year (1910) to advance economic self-help. Many are aware of these two organizations because of black history classes and media discussions. But how many black or white people are aware of the tremendous entrepreneurial activities of African Americans before the civil rights movements of the 1950s and 1960s? In fact, one of the questions the black community should ask itself is why so many of these black businesses have disappeared.

In *Entrepreneurship and Self-Help among Black Americans*, John Sibley Butler gives a very good chronological history of black business enterprise during the early years of America. He discusses black business activities before and after the

Civil War. What is interesting is the amount of black business before World War II and the serious decline after the war. Blacks did best in starting and maintaining their own businesses when the social and political climates were worse for African Americans in America. I discuss why this is so later in this chapter after I give a brief chronology of black entrepreneurship in America.

Anthony Johnson appears to be the first person of African descent to become an entrepreneur in America. He came to this country before the Pilgrims, sometime during the early 1600s. He was not a slave and is documented to have accumulated property in Jamestown, Virginia. Wholesaler and merchant, Jean Baptiste DuSable was one of the earliest settlers of Chicago during this same period. Between 1790 and 1860, only around 10 percent of blacks in America were free. Those who were free had many hostile laws passed against their activity, which restricted what kind of businesses they could operate. Despite this extremely hostile environment, in Pennsylvania, in 1838, a pamphlet entitled "A Registry of Trades of Colored People in the City of Philadelphia and Districts" listed 656 persons engaged in fifty-seven different occupations. It listed bakers, blacksmiths, brass founders, cabinetmakers, and carpenters for the men. Black women ran eighty-one dressmaking and tailoring businesses. Blacks were also engaged in sail making, and one of the most successful was a James Forten, who in 1829 employed forty black and white workers. Steven Smith was a free black man who was a lumber merchant and by the 1850s was grossing over $100,000 annually in sales. Smith was noted to have amassed a net worth of $500,000 by 1864 and was called by some the "king of darkies."[1] Blacks like Robert Bogle controlled the catering business in Philadelphia and made fortunes. There were many more businesses operated by blacks during this time, and they built these businesses in an hostile environment in which they could borrow little, if any, money. Blacks controlled the service businesses during the early years of America. The reason is explained by Abram Harris in *The Negro as Capitalist,* which was published in 1936. Harris stated, "In personal service enterprises the free Negroes had practically no competition. . . . And the fact that white persons tended to avoid enterprises of this character because of their servile status gave free Negroes an advantage in this sphere. Hence, personal service occupations were open freely to black enterprises and constituted a source of considerable income."[2] Today one hears African Americans complain about not having access to capital and protesting to Congress to force banks to loan money to them. Yet during the period before and after the Civil War, blacks organized mutual-aid societies. Most of these mutual-aid societies were run through black churches and were operated as fund-raising membership clubs. Since banks would not lend even to successful black businesses, blacks created their own quasi banks. Until the latter part of this century, blacks found it extremely hard to get life insurance and so started their own insurance companies. The first black insurance company was founded in Philadelphia in 1810 as a response to discrimination by white companies. It was called the African Insurance Company and ran for twenty-three years. By 1932, black insurance companies were operating in twenty-five states and were well established, even though white companies had started to compete strongly with the black companies. Black companies also provided jobs for blacks in insurance, and by 1937, with no opportunities in white companies, 9,000 blacks were employed in black insurance companies.

I could give many more examples of black entrepreneurship in America before 1950, yet today that spirit seems to have been lost. In black communities across America, one sees not African-American entrepreneurs, but Korean or newly arrived immigrants as the entrepreneurs. As I stated earlier, approximately 70 percent of all small business in Los Angeles is owned by Koreans. This is astounding considering the very rich entrepreneurship blacks have had in this country in past years.

BLACK ATTITUDES AND
THE DECLINE OF SELF-HELP

What is the difference between an overachieving racial group like Asian-Americans and underachievers like members of the black underclass? The difference is attitudes: attitudes about life, attitudes about values and success, and most important, attitudes about self. Attitudes explain why some blacks are successful and others are not, even though they grew up in the same neighborhoods. Attitude determines behavior, and behavior determines success or failure. Charles R. Murray, a white conservative social scientist, wrote an interesting article called "White Welfare, White Families, 'White Trash.' "[3] In this piece, Murray points out that there is a "white underclass." This white underclass has remained largely invisible because social scientists are much more interested in blacks. But Murray points out that these poor whites practice some of the same dysfunctional behavior as do the black underclass, behavior like having babies out of wedlock, chronic unemployment, and welfare dependency.[4]

Yet the reasons usually given for the formation of an underclass, such as racism and discrimination, could not possibly be true for these whites.[5] The black middle class, which Murray defines as those making more than $30,000 per year and/or having a college education, share none of the traits or behavior of either the white or the black underclass.[6] Murray argues that education and income are more powerful predictors of social behavior than is race. But what Murray does not discuss is why people acquire this negative behavior and, most crucially, how this behavior can be changed. Why do people act in ways which could be described as underclass? The answer: their beliefs and attitudes. Only when these change will the overall conditions for these people change.

But even with the development of the black underclass, it still remains unclear why blacks aren't more active in business activities. In today's economy, black consumer buying power is over $130 billion, according to a book published by Robert L. Woodson called *On the Road to Economic Freedom*. However, laments Woodson, "Only a tiny fraction of this nation's nearly 15 million businesses is black."[7] In fact, Woodson goes on to say that black business formation is well below that of other ethnic groups. For example, South Central Los Angeles, which was almost totally black in the early 1970s, is now about one-third Latino. Latinos are working in the hundreds of small manufacturing companies that make Los Angeles the nation's leading industrial center. And Latinos, along with a large number of Asians, have taken over most of the gas stations, restaurants, dry-cleaning establishments, and convenience markets on once-black strips such as Central Avenue and Broadway. Paul Hudson, executive vice-president of Broadway Federal Savings and Loan Association—one of Los Angeles's leading minority-owned black-controlled thrifts—says that his business followed the neighborhood's trajectory, all black to 25 percent Latino in only ten years. "There are enormous numbers of

Latino start-ups and Asians buying into existing businesses," observes Hudson, whose family has been active in Los Angeles business for at least sixty years. "They are becoming the owners while the black community is becoming powerless." The remedy, he believes, lies with the thousands of black Americans now working in corporate America, who may be frustrated by their lack of mobility in large companies.[8]

But ironically these corporate types don't want to go into start-up businesses. Says David Abner III, professor of management at Howard University's School of Business, often the best and brightest of the black community are not interested in small-business start-ups: "When you look at those who go to business school, particularly as undergraduates, you're looking at people who want to get into the mainstream by going into corporate America. And in graduate school, a good percentage come from industry and are looking to advance their careers, seeking upward mobility in organizations of which they are already a part."[9] With major corporations actively recruiting minority managers nowadays, he adds, most of his best students prefer opportunities in big business to the risks and headaches of running their own small companies.

But perhaps running a small business would be the best thing to happen to these black business types, because it is still difficult for a black person to rise to the very top of the business world. In an article in *Industry Week*, James Braham states, "Though the opportunities are increasing—in some companies, at least—for blacks, the executive offices remain a small, small world, nothing approaching the 11.7% of the U.S. population or 9.6% of the workforce that blacks represented in the 1980 census."[10] This article goes on to say that blacks account for less than 1 percent of senior executives.

Braham does not argue that the lack of black progress in major corporations is simply racism. Blacks often don't know how to play the corporate game, nor do they have mentors willing to help them. Women executives suffer a fate similar to that of blacks and languish in middle management without getting promoted into the higher ranks.

This dilemma leads black conservatives like Robert Woodson to call on blacks to return to the self-reliance of previous years. As was pointed out earlier, when blacks couldn't work for white insurance companies, they started their own and employed black agents. When blacks couldn't get white bankers to loan them money, they started their own banks, which would. And black undertakers were more than happy to bury blacks who died when white undertakers refused. This in fact is what other ethnic groups are doing. They are starting small businesses in which they employ their own people.

I don't believe affirmative action will move blacks into the boardrooms of America. Also, since most Americans work for small businesses anyway, how would more black executives help black unemployment? I think those blacks who are now frustrated in corporate America should begin to become more entrepreneurial and start businesses. They would not only solve their problem and become, instantly, the head of the board but would also perform a service to the larger black community by hiring blacks as workers. Accomplishing this would be a move away from traditional thinking—that the government ought to do something (though we are seldom clear about what the government ought to do)—and toward the notion that we will do something. Rather than going along the traditional road of attacking racism in corporate America and believing that will be the solution to our problems, we ought to build our own corporations. Once black America did this because it felt it had no other choice. Today many blacks feel there are choices and pursue them instead of self-reliance.

THE FIRST STEP: BUILDING SELF-ESTEEM

The Bible says, "As a man thinketh, so it will be done onto him." But how do you change the way people think? How do you change their fundamental values? Students of psychology will tell you this is not an easy task. Yet it can and must be done. Take, for example, Project Primer in Oakland, California, which is an after-school program that takes fourth- and fifth-graders and exposes them to positive role models. This program uses black and Latino high school and college students to work with these younger kids as group leaders. According to Willie Hamilton, principal of Oakland's Webster Academy, where one of the programs is held, "There have been dramatic changes in attitudes and behavior of the 30 students participating. . . . Some are better able to compete and work."[11] For two and a half hours a day, four days a week, small groups of students meet and discuss mathematics and science. Also, it should be noted that most of the group leaders are males, which seems to have a noticeable effect on the black and Latino boys, according to Hamilton.

An even more drastic approach than Project Primer is the Lock-Up Program run by the First African Methodist Episcopal Church in Los Angeles. This program takes successful African Americans and literally locks them up with young adults for eighteen hours. During this period, the youths are subjected to seminars, speakers, and other activities designed to improve their self-esteem. The University of California, Riverside, has a community outreach program called the Saturday Academy, which stresses building the self-esteem and confidence of African-American youths. These youths meet every other Saturday to discuss leadership and achievement. There are literally hundreds of these small self-help programs all over America. What is surprising is that most of these programs are run by local organizations or individuals and are not necessarily affiliated with or funded by establishment civil rights groups.

The tragedy of the civil rights movement is that, by focusing so much on a redress of grievances, it has virtually ignored the benefits of self-help. None of the affirmative action programs the civil rights community is so vehemently fighting for will help gang members enter legitimate society. Nor will affirmative action persuade a teenage girl not to have a baby. Only respect, pride, and purpose will accomplish this.

Jeffrey Howard, a social psychologist and president of the Efficiency Institute in Lexington, Massachusetts, argues that the key to better schools is motivated students, and that motivation comes from self-respect. He also believes that, if black students believe in themselves, they will try harder, and that, if they try harder, they will succeed. Howard asks a fundamental question: Why do Asians and Jews do well in school while blacks and Hispanics do not? He believes Jews and Asians succeed because they believe they will succeed in school. Blacks and Hispanics do not believe they will be successful in school.[12] Last, Howard believes that personal pride and not just racial pride should be stressed. He feels that pride in self will necessarily lead to pride in race. Howard does raise a valid point about racial versus personal pride. Sometimes a declaration of racial pride can be a mask for feelings of low self-esteem.

Racists can be proud of their race and yet hate themselves. In fact, it can be argued that such self-loathing is one of the root causes of racism. Self-esteem is raised when individuals feel good about themselves; group pride cannot be substituted for individual pride. How to improve self-esteem is a major dilemma for modern America, and not just for blacks. Feelings of low self-esteem, powerlessness, and being disconnected from others are endemic in our society. These feelings cut across racial and ethnic lines, and many white people share similar feelings. Some have argued that the whole "self-help" phenomenon currently sweeping America has done so because people feel disconnected and powerless.

As Harry Edwards, black sports sociologist, has argued, white people can do little to bring about real attitudinal change in the black community. Says Edwards, "There's really nothing white folks can do about illegitimacy in the black community. . . . White society can't deal with its own problems of illegitimacy. That's why we've had 1.7 million abortions in this country since making it legal."[13] Nor does he believe white people can solve the problems in ghetto schools. "There's nothing the white society can do about the problem of a lack of discipline and a lack of competence and a lack of commitment in the black educational system." Edwards believes African Americans have to solve these problems. They have to take the responsibility to generate programs that will provide real solutions because white people have their own problems. "And if we don't," says Edwards, "we are wasting our time whining about what white people didn't do. White people are in a life or death struggle of their own."[14]

The members of the civil rights community argue a

different position from that of Edwards. They argue that it is rampant unemployment in the black community, and not attitudes, which has caused the problems. To the extent that they will admit to the existence of an underclass, they attribute its growth to the rise in unemployment and poverty. Yet researcher Paul Jargowsky found that, while a strong economy boosts black earnings and reduces poverty, it does not reverse negative ghetto practices, such as dropping out of the labor force, out-of-wedlock childbearing, welfare dependency, or crime.[15] If it is not economics or unemployment, then what does sustain the underclass lifestyle? It must be attitudes and values. That's why, according to Harry Edwards, cited earlier, white people can do little to change ghetto schools or to end the cycle of violence in urban areas.

BLACK EMPOWERMENT

During the latter part of the 1960s, many black activists spoke about "black power." Of course in those days this term largely meant social and political power. To some extent African Americans have achieved some political power, which is demonstrated by the clout black voters now exhibit at the polls. Politically, the black community is well organized, compared with other ethnic groups such as Hispanics or Asians. Yet a significant number of African Americans are not empowered. Empowerment means economic and personal power. Economic power is the ability to live a middle-class or higher existence. Personal power is the belief or knowledge that one is at least equal to everyone else in our society. Superachiever groups like Asians (and an earlier ethnic group like Jews) obviously don't feel unequal, which is why they are able to achieve their academic and economic successes.

Black economist and social scientist Thomas Sowell has argued that West Indian blacks share some of the same superachiever traits as Asians and Jews. Sowell attributes this "superachiever" attitude to the culture from which they came, where these blacks saw other blacks in their country in various positions of power. West Indians did not suffer the same personal degradation in their country that American blacks have experienced over the years in America. According to Sowell, their self-esteem is largely intact, which allows them to achieve at higher levels.

How do you raise the self-esteem of African Americans? One approach is the Focus Hope program in Detroit, which successfully helps black men emerge from the underclass. This program is one of the few of its kind. This program trains black men to be machinists, but before they enter the program they must have tenth-grade math and ninth-grade reading. To achieve these scores, the men must attend a lengthy remedial learning program. Through this program, these men learn discipline, but in acquiring discipline, they also learn that anything can be achieved. Black empowerment also comes from owning one's own home. Understanding this imperative, members of Bethel Newlife Church, in a blighted area of Chicago, decided to do something about the housing in the community. Donating just ten dollars per week each, members raised enough money to purchase their first abandoned building, which they turned into condominiums for low-income housing. Most of the residents either are welfare families or earn poverty-level incomes and so can get a down payment to buy their units only through "sweat equity." They do the rehabilitation work themselves. Prospective owners also take turns standing guard at night to keep thieves from stealing the pipes, windows, and refrigerators. Says Bethel Newlife's president, Mary Nelson, "It's the first 'can do' experience for many people and that gives people courage to tackle other things. . . . Once they become homeowners, people begin to care about what's going on in their neighborhood."[16]

PERSONAL PRIDE VERSUS RACE PRIDE

Since the early 1960s, black nationalists have tried to empower black people with statements like "black is beautiful" or "have pride" in your heritage. Yet many African Americans neither act nor feel "beautiful." Why not? Because it is hard to love an abstract concept like a "group" until one truly loves oneself. Teaching racial pride is doomed to fail if one does not teach individual pride and self-respect. Rather than "black power," the call should be for "personal power" or better yet "personal empowerment." Black empowerment will occur when individual blacks start to feel personally powerful, effectual, and in control of their own destinies. Empowering people, any people, is difficult because it cannot be done in mass movements. The programs and self-help groups discussed earlier are all small operations. They work with people in small groups and on an individual basis.

One of the sad facts of life is that in twentieth-century America, most people feel alienated from each other. People need to feel special, and this can only occur in relatively small groups. In fact, at one time in America, black people did feel special. Most blacks lived in rural America, and there was a wide network of extended families and social groups like churches. Even though discriminated against by white society, an individual black person could feel special. Perhaps that is why things appear worse today than thirty or forty years ago. Society as a whole was closer together even though segregated. With the advent of urbanization came alienation, fear, and isolation for all groups, not just blacks. White society has tried to solve its alienation and isolation by creating a plethora of self-help groups, cults, and other organizations. These groups provide "community" for many people.

Blacks need to start many more of the groups discussed earlier. They need to "reinvent" the closeness the black community once had. Today the black underclass is isolated not only from mainstream America, but from middle-class blacks as well. And as middle-class blacks grow older and their parents die, they will lose even more contact with those they left behind. Black empowerment will require a concentrated effort on the part of middle-class blacks to reach the lower classes. It might require a monumental one-on-one effort, but the solution is entirely in black hands.

A CONSERVATIVE BLACK AGENDA?

Black conservatives hold views that are somewhat different than those of white conservatives. They (blacks) oppose affirmative action not because it is racism in reverse, which is why most white conservatives say they oppose it, but because they see it undermining the moral resources that blacks need in order to earn their way into the American mainstream. Their concern is that group-based preferences encourage blacks to look to government largess rather than to self-help and individual initiative.

Black conservatives view integration as a mixed blessing and suggest that it helped put many black enterprises out of business and so undermined the initiative and self-reliance of black communities. They tend to agree with white conservatives that social policies like the welfare system teach dependency. But black conservatives have a bent toward black nationalism and they opposed busing not because it destroyed neighborhood schools, which was the reason given by whites, both conservative and nonconservative. Rather, they opposed busing because they believed it assumed that all-black schools were necessarily inferior.

An example of this is the opinion Supreme Court Justice Clarence Thomas had about *Brown v. Board of Education*. Though he agreed with the result in *Brown* (which overturned the constitutionality of "separate but equal" public schools), he argued that the Court based its reasoning on the notion that black self-esteem and achievement necessarily suffer without the presence of white students.

Black conservatism today is actually a continuation of an old theme in the black community which was first enunciated by men such as Martin R. Delany, a free black man who served in the Union army as the first black captain. After the Civil War, Delany participated in a back-to-Africa movement. He felt that blacks should separate themselves from whites in order to enjoy their newly acquired freedom. As was stated earlier, Marcus Garvey was a black nationalist who headed a strong return-to-Africa movement during the 1920s and actually proposed having blacks return to Africa on steamships that he would acquire. For various reasons neither the Delany nor the Garvey movement was successful in repatriating blacks to Africa, but the ideology that spawned such movements remained. And black leaders such as Malcolm X followed in that ideological tradition.

Black conservatism and black nationalism share many similarities. Both believe that government programs tend to create a certain dependency in blacks and teach them that they are disabled, maimed, and incapable of doing for themselves. This was the teaching of Malcolm X and is the teaching of the Nation of Islam (Black Muslims).

Black conservatives such as Glenn Loury, Shelby Steele, and Thomas Sowell worry that with these government programs blacks have assumed the mantle of victimhood, with its attendant temptations. They believe that American blacks should be focusing their efforts toward building their own businesses and decent homes for themselves as other ethnic groups have done. Black conservatives urge black people, whenever possible, to patronize their own kind, hire their own kind, and start in those ways to build up the black race's ability to do for itself. They feel that this is the only way blacks will get respect and respect themselves.

They also argue that equal standing as a citizen comes from individual effort; that dignity and pride of citizenship in America cannot be conferred politically by affirmative action; that the new path charted for blacks by civil rights leaders and liberals is an experiment that is not working; and that blacks can only make real progress the old-fashioned way—they have got to earn it.

Black conservatives agree with white conservatives that the role of government should be to enforce the rules of fair play, ensure that every child gets a basic education, and then leave individuals to succeed or not on their own. Frederick Douglass, the famous ex-slave, orator, and black Republican, sums it up best in a speech he made several years after the Civil War ended: "All that any man has a right to expect, ask, give or receive in this world, is fair play. When society has secured this to its members, and the humblest citizen of the republic is put into the undisturbed possession of the natural fruits of his own exertions, there is really very little left for society and government to do."[17]

WHAT IS TO BE DONE?

Unfortunately, the neoconservative critique of the current state of black affairs does not provide a course of action for blacks which has not been discussed before. For years African Americans have preached that blacks must help other blacks and return to our basic values, but still we find ourselves in this sorry state of affairs. Middle-class blacks, en masse, have not put forth the kind of effort it will take to help ghetto blacks move ahead. For the most part, these blacks say it is government's responsibility, not theirs, to bring about needed changes in the ghetto. Yet what is behind this apparent indifference by middle-class blacks? Why aren't they more helpful to other less fortunate blacks? Some scholars argue that slavery itself created this class stratification and disunity among blacks by the nature of the slave system. Class stratification occurred when blacks were divided, artificially, between the "field Negroes" and the "house Negroes," according to E. Franklin Frazier. Yet one would be hard-pressed to name any group, even tribal societies, that are not divided along some kind of class lines.

Whatever the reason, the fact remains that African Americans are not, for the most part, as close knit a group as are many other immigrant and ethnic groups. In this context, it becomes clear why "racism," both real and imagined, becomes so important for African Americans to hold onto. It becomes the one defining aspect of the black experience to which all blacks, from former army Chief of Staff General Colin Powell to the lowest black gang member, can relate. Yet for blacks to feel that they are victims of racism and discrimination is not a strong enough concept to bring about the unity that is so desperately needed. Why? Because while Powell and the black gang member share a common heritage of racial discrimination, there is clearly a large difference between how Powell and the gang member have responded to that heritage.

Again, the question remains: Why aren't middle-class blacks more helpful to lower-class blacks? Could it be, despite all the rhetoric to the contrary, that middle-class blacks wish to distance themselves from the lower classes? Are middle-class blacks embarrassed by the behavior of the lower classes? Ellis Cose, the black journalist, said that he outlined the early thesis of his book *The Rage of a Privileged Class* to Senator Daniel Patrick Moynihan. According to Cose, who was writing about black middle-class anger, Moynihan replied, "The black middle class, he (Moynihan) noted, was moving along very well and he had every expectation that it would continue to do so. . . . The big problem is what are we going to do about the underclass? And a particular problem is that [the] black group you're (Cose) talking about [the middle class] doesn't want to have anything to do with them."[18] Was Moynihan right? These questions, painful though they may be, need to be addressed by all African Americans. More empty rhetoric about black unity will not bring about unity if these underlying issues remain.

The self-help concepts and programs discussed earlier are not new. What is new is the urgency and depth of the problems facing lower-class blacks and America as a whole. These problems can be solved only when all blacks come together and have an honest discussion about their own basic beliefs. Middle-class blacks must have the courage to tell the lower classes that their behavior is not desirable and that they (the middle class) resent being stigmatized by lower-class black activities such as crime and out-of-wedlock childbirths. The lower classes must express their anger over being "abandoned" by better-off blacks. They should discuss their resentment of middle-class blacks and how, they feel, these "bourgeois" blacks think themselves better than the lower classes. When this honest dialogue occurs, perhaps African Americans will start being nicer to one another, will create a real bond of unity, and will quit blaming others for problems which only they can solve.

REESTABLISHING BLACK ENTREPRENEURSHIP

Jack Kemp, former secretary of Housing and Urban Development, has been a main proponent of enterprise zones. Federally sponsored enterprise zones are enclaves within depressed areas where business owners and investors receive a variety of federal tax breaks in exchange for starting or expanding operations. The success of these zones is based on the capitalist theory that, given an opportunity for profit, the private sector will do what government has failed to do and turn slum neighborhoods into prosperous communities. Jack Kemp has been the person most out-front on this issue. In 1992, before George Bush left the White House, Kemp told the Senate Finance Committee that "the creation of enterprise zones will instantaneously expand minority entrepreneurship and help bring jobs, prosperity and ownership to people who are today locked into poverty and despair."[19] The concept has been taken up by thirty-eight state governments, and there are now some 2,260 zones scattered across the country—from Boston to San Diego and from Miami to the South Bronx. Kemp claimed they had created almost 260,000 jobs and attracted $28 billion in investment capital "despite the fact that they lack the most powerful ingredient of federal tax incentives, including the ability to reduce such large barriers as the federal income tax, capital gains taxes, payroll taxes and the corporate income tax, which together impose a far higher tax burden than state taxes."[20]

Critics call the numbers on jobs soft and point out that a lot of the jobs were not truly "new" but were simply relocated from other areas. Most important, the critics charge that enterprise zones don't really do much to assist would-be local entrepreneurs in launching new firms. Yet, according to Kemp, that's the main idea. "Our aim" he declares, "is not to lure companies into poor neighborhoods. Our aim is to create new businesses, new jobs and new wealth by getting start-up capital into the hands of low-income entrepreneurs and inner-city residents."[21]

Incredibly, many black experts believe that Kemp's emphasis on fostering minority entrepreneurship is wrongheaded and unrealistic. "Certainly we would like to see indigenous small business development," says Hollis Price, professor of economics at the University of Miami. "But that's going to be extremely difficult in the black community. And if you set that as a task, then you risk always failing. What we want to do is bring some economic life back to these communities, generate employment opportunities. If you can also build up a local business structure, fine. But that's clearly—clearly—a long-term proposition."[22] That is very negative thinking. As was shown earlier, blacks have traditionally had business success, and against incredible odds. Today, because of some of the limited thinking just quoted, black Americans make up about 12 percent of the nation's population, but according to the latest (1990) economic census, only 3 percent of U.S. businesses are black-owned—and they generate a mere 1 percent of total business receipts.

The biggest single obstacle, most experts have argued, is financial capital. But according to economist Constance Dunham, who is studying minority business ownership for the Urban Institute, "Money is not the only thing underpinning business success. You also need training and education and job experience—human capital-type requirements."[23] But we have a great deal of that human capital in the black community. There are blacks who have graduated from business school and become managers. If it isn't capital and it isn't business talent, then it must be attitude. What is lacking in the black community is the will to start up businesses, not the ability.

But we (blacks) get caught up in the belief that government will be our ultimate savior. This is apparent in the rhetoric one hears from educated blacks like David Abner III, professor of management at Howard University, who argues that, if the government really wants to encourage black business ownership, it should establish a Reconstruction Finance Corporation–type investment pool that would be used to finance purchases by local residents of existing white-owned firms in inner-city neighborhoods. That would, among other things, offer bigger opportunities to would-be entrepreneurs with higher skills and better education. And he points out that "although it's true that small business creates most of society's new jobs, small does not really mean the sort of tiny, mom-and-pop retailing or service firms that typically are launched by inexperienced minority businesspeople."[24] This sounds like a great idea, but it will probably not happen just for blacks. Also, look at the immigrant groups, like the Koreans, the Cubans, and even the Mexicans, that have started businesses without the help Abner speaks about. As I said in an earlier chapter, while we (blacks) are waiting around for a government solution such as that Abner proposed, others are moving on and up the ladder.

While we wait, black people continue to be unemployed. Recent U.S. Department of Commerce research shows that black-owned firms hire a significantly higher percentage of black employees than white-owned companies—even those that operate primarily in black areas. But much more important than spawning black business owners is providing training and retraining to give people skills that are now or will be in demand in a high-tech society. The major problem with labor in the inner city, especially among the underclass, is lack of skills. Any segment of the labor force that is unable to keep pace with the rapid changes taking place in technology, in terms of improvement, education, and training, is going to fall further and further behind.

Another issue, raised by William Wilson, is the isolation of the ghetto and the inability of ghetto residents to get to the suburbs, where the jobs increasingly are. Black business ownership would usually be located in the inner cities and therefore accessible to black workers. Another benefit of black business ownership is that it fosters the kind of pride in the community that helps dissuade riots, crime, and other violence. One such example of this pride is Edison Plaza, located in Liberty City, a black section of Miami. Through the use of enterprise zones, a Winn-Dixie Store was built along with 221 housing units, at a total cost of $11 million.

Other local business owners decided to help spruce up the area, and the overall improvement in morale and economic climate has attracted a number of small firms to relocate in the neighborhood from other parts of the city. Perhaps the most revealing sign of the new atmosphere is the fact that when Miami last blew up, in 1989, the Edison Plaza area was spared, while other black communities were burned again. "People know what they have here," says Dewey Knight III, a project manager. "They're very proud of it."[25]

So, though there is much skepticism about how much enterprise zones will do to increase local business ownership, there is no question that some outside firms will be attracted by the zones' tax benefits and other inducements. That's why even many of their critics are willing to see federally backed enterprise zones given a test. "You can't reject alternatives in a vacuum," says Miami's Hollis Price. "If we're going to reject enterprise zones, what are we going to propose to replace them?"[26] Adds Paul Grogan, president of the Local Initiatives Support Corporation, an agency started by the Ford Foundation and now backed by 800 U.S. firms that mainly provide financial aid to local community groups, "Enterprise zones are worth trying, absolutely worth trying. The caution is that they need to be combined with efforts to galvanize the community. To simply offer, in a passive way, varieties of tax relief, is not enough of an inducement to get the private sector to come into these ravaged areas because of the very bad perceptions that surround them and the very real security problems that are frequently there. However, if the community can get organized to take responsibility for its own future, can develop an organization . . . then that more active strategy in combination with tax relief can be useful."[27]

CONCLUSION

William Raspberry once wrote, "We speak of income gaps, education gaps, test-score gaps, even life-span gaps, not merely to describe but to accuse. The gaps are proof of racism, and the government ought to do something to close them. The problem with this approach is that it puts the remedies to black America's problems outside black America. It encourages the belief that to attack racism as the cause of our problem is the same as attacking our problems. And so we expend precious resources—time, energy, imagination, political capital—searching (always successfully) for evidence of racism, while our problems grow worse."[28]

I quote Raspberry because none of the above solutions will work until blacks understand his sentiments. What has stopped black business entrepreneurship is lack of interest by blacks, not racism. We would rather spend our time, energy, and political capital on trying to get minority business set-asides than on starting businesses. Racism does exist. It exists at the higher levels of corporate America, but what should be black America's response? Should we try to force General Motors to make its next CEO a black or work to open up more black auto dealerships? How does one get money to open up a dealership? By obtaining a loan from a black bank perhaps, or by getting money from black churches. These are only examples of what might be done. But clearly, if energy is going to be expended, it should be used to move things into the black community's control and not into the control of others.

CHAPTER NINE

Conclusion: Racial Healing

Black Americans have been in America for almost 400 years. They endured 250 years of legal slavery and another 100 years of legal segregation. It has been only since the early 1960s that legalized segregation has been abolished. Yet the mental scars of those years of slavery and oppression have not been completely overcome by blacks. The Thirteenth Amendment, which freed the slaves, has language that both frees the slaves physically and also tries to remove the "badges of servitude" from the former slaves. I don't believe those "badges of servitude" have ever completely left African Americans. I believe blacks are still recovering from the aftermath of slavery and, in a real sense, remain dependent on white America for survival. I think this dependency also causes conflicts and represents a "love–hate" relationship. I say *love–hate* because black America needs validation from whites that it is OK but resents the need for that validation. Since that validation has to come from "outside the self," it never comes. Ellis Cose's middle-class blacks who felt like outsiders even though they had everything America has to offer in terms of material wealth will always feel "outside." These middle-class blacks are looking for validation, a pat on the back, by white America which says, "You are OK." I believe it is time for these middle-class blacks and indeed all blacks to "pat" themselves on the back and say, "We are OK." This is what I call racial healing.

White America also needs racial healing. There are still lingering vestiges of racism that require a purging. And racial polarization has become a problem today because whites and blacks don't speak to one another, and when they do, it is from such different experiences and motives that no meaningful dialogue takes place. It's as though there were two languages of race in America.

Blacks and whites differ on their interpretations of social change from the 1960s through the 1990s because their racial languages define the central terms—especially racism—differently. Their racial languages incorporate different views of American society itself, especially the question of how central race and racism are to America's very existence, past and present. Blacks see race as all-important, while most whites, except for the most race-conscious, see race as a peripheral reality. Even the most successful middle-class black professionals, as stated earlier, fear racial slights or humiliations. They are extremely concerned about incidents which may occur when they are stopped by police, or are regarded suspiciously by clerks while shopping, or are mistaken for messengers, drivers, or aides at work. Whether these things have ever happened to them or not, it is still a fear which causes them to exude, as William Raspberry says, "a mild form of paranoia." White people don't understand this. For whites, race becomes central only on exceptional occasions, collective, public moments such as the Rodney

King beating and the aftermath of riots, or when the family decides to escape urban problems with a move to the suburbs. But most of the time whites are able to view racial issues as aberrations in American life, much as Los Angeles police chief Daryl Gates used the term *aberration* to explain his officers' beating of Rodney King in March 1991.

Because of these differences in language and worldview, blacks and whites often talk past one another, particularly during discussions of racism. Whites locate racism in color consciousness and its absence in color blindness. For whites it is an absence of color consciousness that determines whether racism exists. For blacks color blindness is not possible since race is so important to them. Racism, as I argued earlier, is a very central theme in the lives of black people. It explains black failure and success. It explains ghetto life and rising crime statistics. In an interesting 1993 article called "Language of Race: Talking Past One Another," Bob Blauner, professor of sociology at Berkeley, says, "Whites saw racism largely as a thing of the past. They defined it in terms of segregation and lynching, explicit white supremacist beliefs, or double standards in hiring, promotion, and admissions to colleges or other institutions. Except for affirmative action, which seemed the most blatant expression of such double standards, they were positively impressed by racial change. Many saw the relaxed and comfortable relations between whites and blacks as the heart of the matter. More crucial to blacks, on the other hand, were the underlying structures of power and position that continued to provide them with unequal portions of economic opportunity and other possibilities for the good life."[1]

White people have never been able to understand the

expanded definitions of *racism* that blacks give to the word. *Institutional racism* is a concept many whites do not see because it is hard to imagine entire institutions as racist. For blacks, these concepts are not hard to understand because race is such an important aspect of black consciousness. Whites are more likely than blacks to view racism as a personal issue. Both sensitive to their own possible culpability (if only unconsciously) and angry at the use of the concept of racism by angry minorities, they do not differentiate well between the racism of social structures and the accusation that they as participants in those structures are personally racist. White people resent the notion of collective guilt and resist the idea that, because their ancestors may have benefited from black disenfranchisement, they are personally guilty.

The idea of collective guilt has meaning for blacks, and they feel whites ought to be sorry about how blacks were treated. This is the rationale blacks use for affirmative action. While whites see affirmative action as "reverse discrimination," blacks see it as reparation or a payback for past injustices. The black neoconservative movement has largely moved away from this position. Many blacks have sensed that too heavy an emphasis on racism has led to the false conclusion that blacks can progress only through a conventional civil rights strategy of fighting prejudice and discrimination. Overemphasizing racism, they fear, has been interfering with the black community's ability to achieve greater self-determination through the politics of self-help. In addition, they believe that the prevailing rhetoric of the 1960s affected many young blacks. Rather than taking responsibility for their own difficulties, they are now using racism as a "cop-out."

RACE CONSCIOUSNESS

Part of the job of racial healing in America is to reduce the obsession with race. In the American consciousness, the imagery of race—especially along the black–white dimension—tends to be more powerful than that of class or ethnicity. As a result, legitimate ethnic affiliations are often misunderstood to be racial and illegitimate. Race itself is a confusing concept because of the variance between scientific and commonsense definitions of the term. Physical anthropologists who study the distribution of those characteristics we use to classify "races" teach us that race is a fiction because all peoples are mixed to various degrees. Sociologists counter that this biological fiction unfortunately remains a sociological reality. People define one another racially and thus divide society into racial groups. The "fiction" of race affects every aspect of people's lives, from living standards to landing in jail. The consciousness of color differences and the invidious distinctions based on them have existed since antiquity and are not limited to any one corner of the world. And yet the peculiarly modern division of the world into a discrete number of hierarchically ranked races is a historical product of Western colonialism. In precolonial Africa, the relevant group identities were national, tribal, or linguistic. There was no concept of an African or black people until this category was created by the combined effects of slavery, imperialism, and the anticolonial and Pan-African movements. The legal definitions of blackness and whiteness, which have varied from one society to another in the Western hemisphere, have also been crucial to the construction of modern-day races. Thus race is an essentially political construct, one that translates our tendency to see people in

terms of their color or other physical attributes into structures that make it likely that people will act for or against
them on this basis.

The dynamic of ethnicity is different, even though the
results may at times be similar. An ethnic group is a group
that shares a belief in its common past. Members of an ethnic
group hold a set of common memories that make them feel
that their customs, culture, and outlook are distinctive. In
short, they have a sense of peoplehood. Sharing critical
experiences and sometimes a belief in their common fate,
they feel an affinity for one another, a "comfort zone" that
leads to congregating together, even when this congregating
is not forced by exclusionary barriers. Thus, if race is associated with biology and nature, ethnicity is associated with
culture. Like races, ethnic groups arise historically, transform themselves, and sometimes die out.

Much of the popular discourse about race in America
today goes awry because ethnic realities get lost under the
racial umbrella. The positive meanings and potential of ethnicity are overlooked—even overrun—by the more inflammatory meanings of race. Thus white students on today's
colleges campuses become disturbed when blacks associate
with each other and justify their objections through their
commitment to racial integration. In fact, to these white
students, blacks are practicing a kind of reverse racism.
They do not appreciate the ethnic affinities that bring this
about or see the parallels to Jewish students' meeting at
the campus Hillel Foundation or Italian-Americans' eating
lunch at the Italian house on the campus of the University
of California at Berkeley.

When blacks are "being ethnic," says Bob Blauner,
whites see them as "being racial." Thus they view the identity politics of students who want to celebrate their black-

ness, their chicanoismo, their Asian heritage, and their Native American roots as racially offensive. Part of this reaction comes from a sincere desire, on the part of white students, for a color-blind society. But, states Blauner, "because the ethnicity of darker people so often gets lost in our over-racialized perceptions, the white students misread the situation. When I point out to my class that whites are talking about race and its dynamics and the students of color are talking about ethnicity and its differing meaning, they can begin to appreciate each other's agendas."[2] A start along the road of racial healing would be for whites and blacks to better understand one another in regard to race and ethnicity.

RACIAL VULNERABILITY

While whites need a better understanding of race and ethnicity, blacks are most in need of racial healing. How do blacks become racially healed? By allowing themselves to believe that all things in life are not determined by race and letting go of race as a defining concept. Doing this will make blacks, I believe, more vulnerable to a possibly racist society. But it will liberate blacks because it will force them to respond to people as individuals and not as representatives of a race. I think the problem with black attitudes about whites is that blacks see whites as some "giant omnipotent" race of people against whom blacks, like David in the Bible, must fight. As I said earlier, white people have numerous problems, inferiority complexes, weaknesses, and failings, as do all peoples. White people, like blacks, put their socks on "one foot at a time." When blacks start to see white people in these more human, vulnerable terms, then blacks will be

able to take them "one person at a time" rather than as
a race.

BLACK POWER

The great challenge facing blacks today is the task of
taking control of their own future by exerting the necessary
leadership, making the required sacrifices, and building the
needed institutions so that black social and economic development becomes a reality. No matter what debates occur in
our society over what should be done, the solution is solely
in black hands. Black power is opposed to the notion that
black people must sit and wait for white Americans, of
whatever political persuasion, to come to their rescue.

Blacks must take a less adversarial tone in their dealings with white America. In situations where affirmative
action may be appropriate, it should be based not on race,
but on economic class. This will reduce the racial polarization and develop a broader support among all Americans.
Blacks must argue a win-win public policy and not "We
win" because we are oppressed and "You lose" because you
somehow share a collective guilt. No people want to be
losers in our society, nor should they be.

Last, the drive for integration must be modified to the
extent that it does not undermine black institutions. It will
be black institutions that will ultimately help us solve the
problems in the black community. A racially healed black
community will not need to use racism as an excuse for not
being more successful.

Racially healed blacks will be able to work with whites
in a less adversarial environment because they (blacks) will
no longer need to manipulate whites, through "guilt trips,"

in order to get what they want. And what racially healed blacks will want will be not a "race-specific" public policy, but a policy designed to help all Americans in need of special services. Affirmative action would mean helping those of any race who come from economically disadvantaged backgrounds.

Finally, racially healed blacks will be able to build coalitions between different groups and races. These coalitions will aid in creating a more equitable public policy for the poor and the disadvantaged in America. And ultimately, these racially healed blacks will understand that it is they who will solve the problems of black America and not some outside force.

Notes

Introduction

1. Daniel P. Moynihan, *The Negro Family: The Case for National Action* (Washington, DC: Office of Policy Planning and Research, U.S. Department of Labor, 1965), p. 113.
2. U.S. Bureau of the Census, *Current Population Reports*, "Household and Family Characteristics (Sept. 1992).
3. Ibid.
4. U.S. Department of Justice, *Uniform Crime Reports for the United States, 1990* (Washington, DC: Government Printing Office, 1990).
5. U.S. Department of Commerce, *U.S. Statistical Abstracts 1993* (Washington, DC: Government Printing Office).
6. U.S. Bureau of the Census, *Current Population Reports* (Sept. 1992).
7. William Julius Wilson, *The Truly Disadvantaged* (Chicago: University of Chicago Press, 1987).
8. Sam Roberts, *Who We Are* (New York: Times Books, 1993).
9. Ibid., p. 109.
10. U.S. Bureau of the Census, *Current Population Reports, 1970; 1980* (Sept. 1992).
11. Ibid. When comparing census data over ten-year intervals, one can see growth of the black middle class.
12. Thomas B. Edsalls and Mary D. Edsalls, *Chain Reaction: The Impact of Race, Rights, and Taxes in American Politics* (New York: Norton, 1992).
13. Joseph Perkins in the *San Diego Union* (Oct. 2, 1990). This quote was obtained from "The Role of Racism in Black Poverty Is Exaggerated,"

by William Raspberry, in an anthology, *Racism*, edited by David L. Bender and Bruno Leone (San Diego: Greenhaven Press, 1991), p. 97.

14. U.S. Bureau of the Census, *Current Population Reports* (Sept. 1992).

15. U.S. Department of Justice, *Uniform Crime Reports for the United States, 1994* (Washington, DC: U.S. Government Printing Office).

16. A review of census and crime statistics shows that these data are growing worse for blacks over time.

17. For an excellent discussion of conditions in black America, see St. Clair Drake and Horace Cayton, *Black Metropolis: A Study of Negro Family Life in a Northern City*, Vol. 2 (New York: Harper & Row, 1945), and E. Franklin Frazier, *The Negro Family in the United States* (Chicago: University of Chicago Press, 1937).

18. William Julius Wilson, *The Declining Significance of Race* (Chicago: University of Chicago Press, 1978), p. 23.

19. Wilson, *The Truly Disadvantaged*.

20. Ibid.

21. Ibid.

22. Alan Grimshaws, *A History of Racial Conflict in America* (Stanford, CA: Stanford University Press, 1975).

23. U.S. Department of Justice, *Uniform Crime Reports for the United States, 1994* (Washington, DC: U.S. Government Printing Office).

24. Thomas Sowell, *Civil Rights: Rhetoric or Reality?* (New York: William Morrow, 1984), pp. 13–14. Also see Wilson, *The Truly Disadvantaged*, pp. 20–21.

25. Wilson, *The Truly Disadvantaged*, p. 21.

26. Ibid., pp. 20–30.

27. Ibid.

28. Ibid.

29. J. A. Parker, "The Rising Black Middle Class Proves Racism Is in Decline." In *Racism*, ed. David L. Bender and Bruno Leone (San Diego: Greenhaven Press, 1991), p. 96.

30. Ibid.

31. Wilson, *The Truly Disadvantaged*, p. 21.

32. U.S. Bureau of the Census, *Current Population Reports* (Sept. 1992).

33. Bart Landry, *The New Black Middle Class* (Berkeley: University of California Press, 1987).

34. Parker, "The Rising Black Middle Class."

35. The Urban Institute report appeared in *New Republic* (June 10, 1991), p. 7, "In black and white" (editorial).

36. William Raspberry, "The Role of Racism in Black Poverty Is Exagge-

rated." In *Racism*, David L. Bender and Bruno Leone (San Diego: Greenhaven Press, 1991), p. 87.

37. Ibid., p. 88.

Chapter 1

1. Bob Blauner, "Language of Race: Talking Past One Another," *Current* (Jan. 1993), p. 4.

2. Nicholas Lemann, "The Origins of the Underclass." *Washington Monthly* (June 1986).

3. Ibid.

4. Glenn Loury, *Love and Loathing*, ed. Gerald Early (Viking Press, 1992).

5. Joseph Epstein, "Today's Professional Victims," *Reader's Digest* (April 1991).

6. Wayne Edwards, "Going It Alone," interview with Shelby Steele, *People's Weekly*, (Sept. 2, 1993), p. 74.

7. Dennis Prager, "Blacks and Liberals: The Los Angeles Riots," (Jan. 1993), p. 11. Hooks is quoted in this article.

8. Ibid. Vivian Gordon is quoted in this article.

9. Ibid.

10. Ellis Cose, *The Rage of a Privileged Class* (New York: HarperCollins, 1994).

11. Ibid.

12. Ibid.

13. Prager, "Blacks and Liberals."

14. Ibid.

15. Ibid.

16. Ibid.

17. Ibid.

18. Ibid.

19. Ibid.

20. Ibid.

21. Ibid.

22. Ibid.

23. Shelby Steele talks about this during his college days and how he was able to make liberal white students feel guilty. I had similar experiences while attending college.

24. Prager, "Blacks and Liberals."

25. Ibid.
26. Ibid.
27. Ibid.
28. Ibid.
29. Ibid.
30. Ibid.
31. Thomas Sowell, *Civil Rights: Rhetoric or Reality?* (New York: William Morrow, 1984), p. 77.
32. William Raspberry, "The Role of Racism in Black Poverty Is Exaggerated." In *Racism*, David L. Bender and Bruno Leone (San Diego: Greenhaven Press, 1991), p. 89.
33. U.S. Department of Justice, *Uniform Crime Reports for the United States, 1991* (Washington, DC: U.S. Government Printing Office).

Chapter 2

1. William Julius Wilson, *The Truly Disadvantaged* (Chicago: University of Chicago Press, 1987), pp. 7–8.
2. Ibid., pp. 180–184.
3. Ibid.
4. Charles Murray, *Losing Ground: American Social Policy 1950–1980* (New York: Basic Books, 1984), p. 68.
5. Wilson, *The Truly Disadvantaged*.
6. Ibid.
7. Ibid.
8. Daniel P. Moynihan, *The Negro Family: The Case for National Action* (Washington, DC: Office of Policy Planning and Research, U.S. Department of Labor, 1965).
9. Wilson, *The Truly Disadvantaged*.
10. Ibid.
11. Herbert Gans, "Culture and Class in the Study of Poverty: An Approach to Antipoverty Research." In *On Understanding Poverty: Perspectives from the Social Sciences*, ed. Daniel Patrick Moynihan (New York: Basic Books, 1968).
12. Wilson, *The Truly Disadvantaged*.
13. Ibid.

14. Derrick Bell, *Faces at the Bottom of the Well* (New York: Basic Books, 1992).
15. Alvin F. Poussaint, "The Price of Success," *Ebony* (Aug. 1987), p. 70.
16. Nathan Hare, "Is the Black Middle Class Blowing It?" *Ebony* (Aug. 1987), p. 85.
17. Ellis Cose, "The Price of Assimilation," *Newsweek* (July 11, 1994).
18. Ibid.
19. J.A. Parker, "The Rising Black Middle Class Proves Racism Is in Decline." In *Racism*, eds. David L. Bender and Bruno Leone (San Diego: Greenhaven Press, 1991), p. 96.
20. The Rodney King incident involved four white police officers who beat a black motorist, Rodney King, while attempting to arrest him. The beating was filmed on videotape and became famous. The four police officers were tried before a nearly all-white jury and found innocent. This verdict sparked a riot.
21. Wilson, *The Truly Disadvantaged*.
22. Ibid.

Chapter 3

1. William A. Henry III, "What Price Preference? (Affirmative Action)," *Time* (Sept. 30, 1991) p. 30.
2. Stephen Carter, *Reflections of an Affirmative Action Baby* (New York: Basic Books, 1991).
3. Stanley Fish, "Reverse Racism or How the Pot Got to Call the Kettle Black," *Atlantic* (Nov. 1993) p. 128.
4. Henry, "What Price Preference?"
5. Ibid.
6. Elena Neuman, "The Right Arises in Black Politics," *Insight* (Sept. 27, 1993), p. 6.
7. Silvester Monroe, "Does Affirmative Action Help or Hurt? Black Conservatives Say Their People Become Addicted to Racial Preferences Instead of Hard Work," *Time* (May 27, 1991), p. 22.
8. Ibid.
9. Ibid.
10. Henry, "What Price Preference?"
11. Ibid.

12. Ibid.
13. Ronald A. Taylor, "Why Fewer Blacks Are Graduating," *U.S. News and World Report* (June 8, 1987), p. 75.
14. Set-asides have to do with with preferential hiring and promotion.
15. Tamar Jacoby, "Psyched Out: Why Black Students Feel Torn," *New Republic* (Feb. 18, 1991), p. 28.
16. Ibid.
17. Wayne Edwards, "Going It Alone," interview with Shelby Steele, in *People's Weekly* (Sept. 2, 1993), p. 74.
18. Lino A. Graglia, "Affirmative Discrimination," *National Review* (July 5, 1993), p. 26.
19. Taylor, "Why Fewer Blacks Are Graduating."
20. Dinesh D'Souza, "Sins of Admission: Affirmative Action on Campus," *New Republic* (Feb. 18, 1991), p. 30.
21. Taylor, "Why Fewer Blacks Are Graduating."
22. Michel Marriott, "Intense College Recruiting Drives Lifts Black Enrollment to a Record," *New York Times* (April 15, 1990).
23. Laurel Shaper Walters, "More Blacks in US Colleges," *Christian Science Monitor* (April 3, 1990).
24. Ibid.
25. Marriott, "College Recruiting Drives Lifts Black Enrollment," *New York Times* (April 15, 1990).
26. Ibid.
27. Taylor, "Why Fewer Blacks Are Graduating."
28. Ibid.
29. Henry, "What Price Preference?"

Chapter 4

1. William Tucker, "Is Police Brutality the Problem?" (Jan. 1993), p. 23.
2. Ibid.
3. Ibid.
4. Ibid.
5. Coramae Richie Mann, *Unequal Justice: A Question of Color* (Indiana: University Press, 1993).
6. Les Payne, "Up against the Wall: Black Men and the Cops," *Essence* (Nov. 1992), p. 72.

7. Ibid.
8. Paul Glastris and Jeannye Thornton, "A New Civil Rights Frontier: After His Own Home and Neighborhood Were Invaded by Street Punks, Jesse Jackson Dedicated Himself to Battling Black-on-Black Crime," *U.S. News and World Report* (Jan. 17, 1994), p. 38.
9. Ibid.
10. Ibid.
11. Ibid.
12. Ted Gest, "Why Brutality Persists: There Would Be Much Less of a Problem If Bad Cops Weren't Coddled," *U.S. News and World Report* (Apr. 1, 1991), p. 24.
13. Tucker, "Is Police Brutality the Problem?"
14. Richard Lacayo, "Law and Disorder: For Cops, Fear and Frustration Are Constants. Sometimes Even the Best of Them Snap under Pressure," *Time* (Apr. 1, 1991), p. 18.
15. Ibid.
16. Gordon Witkin, "Cops under Fire," *U.S. News and World Report* (Dec. 3, 1990), p. 32.
17. Tucker, "Is Police Brutality the Problem?"
18. Ibid.
19. Witkin, "Cops under Fire."
20. Ibid.
21. Ibid.
22. Ibid.
23. Ibid.
24. Lacayo, "Law and Disorder."
25. Ibid.
26. Ibid.
27. Gest, "Why Brutality Persists."
28. Witkin, "Cops under Fire."

Chapter 5

1. Jonathan Kaufman, "Broken Alliance: The Turbulent Times between Blacks and Jews in America." (book review) *Washington Monthly* (Nov. 1988), p. 51.

2. John Hope Franklin, *From Slavery to Freedom* (New York: Vintage Books, 1969), pp. 218–220.
3. Lance Morrow, "The Provocative Professor," *Time* (Aug. 26, 1991), p. 19.
4. Ibid.
5. David Kurapka, "Hate Story: Farrakhan's Still at It," *New Republic* (May 30, 1988), p. 19.
6. Ibid.
7. Ibid.
8. Jonathan Brent, "Political Perversity in Chicago: Why the Sudden Outburst of Race Hate," *New Republic* (Aug. 8, 1988), p. 16.
9. Ibid.
10. Ibid.
11. Richard Brookhiser, "Fear and Loathing at City College," *National Review* (June 11, 1990), p. 20.
12. Ibid.
13. Jonathan Rieder, "Crown of Thorns: The Roots of the Black–Jewish Feud," *New Republic* (Oct. 14, 1991), p. 26.
14. Ibid.
15. A good discussion regarding black middle-class attitudes about opening businesses in the ghetto is in Dan Cordtz, "Mainstreaming the Ghetto," *Financial World* (Sept. 1, 1992), p. 22.
16. Chris Herlinger, "Culture Clash," *Scholastic Update* (March 20, 1992), p. 16.
17. Ibid.
18. Jonathan Rieder, "Trouble in Store: Behind the Brooklyn Boycott," *New Republic* (July 2, 1990), p. 16.
19. Ibid.
20. Ibid.
21. Ibid.
22. Ibid.
23. Ibid.
24. Ibid.
25. Ibid.
26. Herlinger, "Culture Clash."
27. Rieder, "Trouble in Store."
28. Ibid.
29. Ibid.
30. Ibid.

31. Cordtz, "Mainstreaming the Ghetto."
32. Ibid.
33. Jack Miles, "Blacks vs. Browns," *Atlantic* (Oct. 1992), p. 41.
34. Ibid.
35. Nicholas Lemann, "The Other Underclass," *Atlantic* (Dec. 1991), p. 96.
36. Ibid.
37. Ibid.
38. Ibid.
39. Jacob V. Lamar, "A Brightly Colored Tinderbox: Miami's Latest Riot Highlights Tensions between Immigrants and Native-Born Blacks," *Time* (Jan. 30, 1989), p. 28.
40. Ibid.
41. Ibid.
42. Ibid.
43. Ibid.

Chapter 6

1. Charles Murray, *Losing Ground: American Social Policy 1950–1980* (New York: Basic Books, 1984), p. 68.
2. Ibid.
3. Mickey Kaus, "The Work Ethic State: The Only Way to Break the Culture of Poverty," *New Republic* (July 7, 1986), p. 22.
4. Ibid.
5. Quoted from a 1994 program on public television regarding President Clinton's pending welfare legislation.
6. Ibid.
7. Howard Gleckman and Paul Magnusson, "Reforming Welfare," *Business Week* (June 13, 1994), p. 62.
8. Kaus, "The Work Ethic State."
9. Richard A. Cloward and Frances Fox Piven, "A Class Analysis of Welfare," *Monthly Review* (Feb. 1993), p. 25.
10. Ibid.
11. Ibid.
12. Dante Ramos, "Kvetch, Kvetch," *New Republic* (Apr. 25, 1994), pp. 24–25.
13. Ibid.

14. Ibid.
15. Marshall Ingwerson, "As Clinton Team Prepares Drafts, States Are Off, Running on Welfare," *Christian Science Monitor* (March 2, 1994), p. 4.
16. Kaus, "The Work Ethic State."
17. Cloward and Piven, "A Class Analysis of Welfare."
18. Ramos, "Kvetch, Kvetch."
19. Gleckman and Magnusson, "Reforming Welfare."
20. Kaus, "The Work Ethic State."
21. Ibid.
22. Ibid.

Chapter 7

1. Juan Williams, Roger Wilkins, and Kristen L. Hays, "Integration Turns 40: The New Segregation," *Modern Maturity* (April–May 1994), p. 24.
2. Ibid.
3. Ibid.
4. James Traub, "Separate and Equal," *Atlantic* (Sept. 1991), p. 24.
5. Ibid.
6. James Traub, "Ghetto Blasters: The Case for All-Black Schools," *New Republic* (Apr. 15, 1991), p. 21.
7. Ibid.
8. Ibid.
9. Ibid.
10. Ibid.
11. Ibid.
12. Ibid.
13. Ibid.
14. Stephen Macedo, "Douglass to Thomas: The Roots of Black Conservatism," *New Republic* (Sept. 30, 1991), p. 23.
15. Ibid.
16. Ibid.
17. Ibid.
18. Elena Neuman, "The Right Arises in Black Politics," *Insight* (Sept. 27, 1993), p. 6
19. Ibid.

20. Ibid.
21. Ibid.
22. Joel Kotkin, "A New Black Dream," *Inc.* (Nov. 1989), p. 30.
23. Neuman, "The Right Arises in Black Politics."
24. Ibid.
25. Ibid.
26. Ibid.
27. Ibid.
28. Ibid.
29. Ibid.
30. Ibid.
31. Ibid.
32. Ibid.
33. Ibid.
34. Ibid.
35. Ibid.
36. Ibid.
37. Ibid.
38. Ibid.
39. Ibid.
40. Ibid.
41. Ibid.
42. Ibid.
43. Ibid.
44. Ibid.
45. Ibid.
46. Ibid.
47. Ibid.
48. Ibid.
49. A quote of W. E. B. DuBois in Glenn Loury, "Making It All Happen." In *On the Road to Economic Freedom*, ed. Robert L. Woodson (Washington, D.C.: Regnery Gateway, 1987), p. 116.
50. Glenn Loury, "Making It All Happen," p. 177.

Chapter 8

1. John Sibley Butler, *Entrepreneurship and Self-Help among Black Americans* (New York: State University of New York, 1991).

2. Ibid.
3. Charles R. Murray, "White Welfare, White Families, 'White Trash,'" *National Review* (March 28, 1986), p. 36.
4. Ibid.
5. Ibid.
6. Charles Murray, *Losing Ground: American Social Policy 1950–1980* (New York: Basic Books, 1984).
7. Robert L. Woodson, "A Legacy of Entrepreneurship." In *On the Road to Economic Freedom*, ed. Robert L. Woodson (Washington, DC: Regnery Gateway, 1987).
8. Joel Kotkin, "A New Black Dream," *Inc.* (Nov. 1989), p. 30.
9. Cordtz, "Mainstreaming the Ghetto," *Financial World* (Sept. 1, 1992).
10. James Braham, "Is the Door Really Open? Outright Bias Is Disappearing but Now the Few Black Executives Nearing the Top Must Overcome the 'Comfort' Barrier," *Industry Week* (Nov. 16, 1987), p. 64.
11. Susan Mandel, "Taking Matters into Their Own Hands," *National Review* (March 28, 1990), p. 65.
12. Ibid.
13. Michael Covino, "The Unpopular Voice of Black Realism," *Whole Earth Review* (Fall 1988), p. 28.
14. Ibid.
15. David Whitman, "The Shifting State of Black Ghettoes: A New Study Answers Some Big Questions," *U.S. News and World Report* (Jan. 18, 1993), p. 33.
16. Mandel, "Taking Matters into Their Own Hands."
17. Elena Neuman, "The Right Arises in Black Politics," *Insight* (Sept. 27, 1993).
18. Ellis Cose, *The Rage of a Privileged Class* (New York: HarperCollins, 1994).
19. Cordtz, "Mainstreaming the Ghetto."
20. Ibid.
21. Ibid.
22. Ibid.
23. Ibid.
24. Ibid.
25. Ibid.
26. Ibid.
27. Ibid.

28. William Raspberry, "The Role of Racism in Black Poverty Is Exaggerated." In *Racism*, eds. David L. Bender and Bruno Leone (San Diego: Greenhaven Press, 1991).

Chapter 9

1. Bob Blauner, "Language of Race: Talking Past One Another," *Current* (Jan. 1993), p. 4.
2. Ibid.

Bibliography

Anderson, Martin, *Welfare* (Stanford, CA: Hoover Institute Press, 1978).

Auletta, K., *The Underclass* (New York: Random House, 1982).

Banfield, E., *The Unheavenly City Revisited* (Boston: Little, Brown, 1976).

Bender, D. L., and B. Leone (eds.), *Racism* (San Diego: Greenhaven Press, 1991).

Billingsly, A., *Black Families in White America* (Englewood Cliffs, NJ: Prentice-Hall, 1969).

Butler, J. S., *Entrepreneurship and Self-Help among Black Americans* (New York: State University of New York, 1991).

Carter, S. L., *Reflections of an Affirmative Action Baby* (New York: Basic Books, 1991).

Clark, K., *Dark Ghetto: Dilemmas of Social Power* (New York: Harper & Row, 1965).

Cose, Ellis, *The Rage of a Privileged Class* (New York: HarperCollins, 1994).

Drake, St. C., and H. Cayton, *Black Metropolis: A Study of Negro Family Life in a Northern City*, Vol. 2 (New York: Harper & Row, 1945).

Edsalls, T. B., and M. D. Edsalls, *Chain Reaction: The Impact of Race, Rights and Taxes in American Politics* (New York: Norton, 1992).

Early, Gerald (ed.), *Love and Loathing* (New York: Viking Press, 1992).

Fishman, L. (ed.), *Poverty and Affluence* (New Haven, CT: Yale University Press, 1966).

Franklin, J. H., *From Slavery to Freedom* (New York: Vintage Books, 1969).

Frazier, E. Franklin, *The Negro Family in the United States* (Chicago: University of Chicago Press, 1937).

Gans, Herbert, "Culture and Class in the Study of Poverty: An Approach to Antipoverty Research." In *On Understanding Poverty: Perspectives from the Social Sciences*, ed. Daniel Patrick Moynihan (New York: Basic Books, 1968).

Gilder, George, *Wealth and Poverty* (New York: Basic Books, 1981).

Glazer, Nathan, *The Limits of Social Policy* (Cambridge MA: Harvard University Press, 1971).

Gordon, M. M., "Toward a General Theory of Racial and Ethnic Group Relations." In *Ethnicity, Theory and Experience*, eds. N. Glazer and D. P. Moynihan (Cambridge, MA: Harvard University Press, 1975).

Grimshaws, Alan, *A History of Racial Conflict in America* (Stanford, CA: Stanford University Press, 1975).

Katz, Irwin, and R. Glen Hass, "Racial Ambivalence and American Value Conflict: Correlational and Priming Studies of Dual Cognitive Structures," *Journal of Personality and Social Psychology*, 1988.

Kaus, Mickey, *The End of Equality* (New York: Basic Books, 1992).

Kluegel, James R., "Trends in Whites' Explanations of the Black–White Gap in Socio-economic Status, 1977–1989," *American Sociological Review* (August 1990).

Landry, Bart, *The New Black Middle Class* (Berkeley, CA: University of California Press, 1987).

Liebow, E., *Talley's Corner: A Study of Negro Street-Corner Men* (Boston: Little, Brown, 1967).

Mead, L., *Beyond Entitlement: The Social Obligation of Citizenship* (New York: Free Press, 1986).

Mead, L., *The New Politics of Poverty* (New York: Basic Books, 1992).

Moynihan, D. P., "The Negro Family: The Case for National Action" (Washington, DC: Office of Policy Planning and Research, U.S. Department of Labor, 1965).

Moynihan, D. P., and N. Glazer, *Beyond the Melting Pot* (Cambridge, MA: MIT Press, 1963).

Murray, C., *Losing Ground: American Social Policy, 1950–1980* (New York: Basic Books, 1984).

Piven, F. F., and R. A. Cloward, *Regulating the Poor: The Functions of Public Welfare* (New York: Academic Press, 1971).

Rainwater, L., "Crucible of Identity: The Negro Lower Class Family," *Daedalus* (Winter 1966), pp. 176–216.

Roberts, Sam, *Who We Are* (New York: Times Books, 1993).

Sowell, Thomas, *Civil Rights: Rhetoric or Reality?* (New York: William Morrow, 1984).

Steele, S., *The Content of Our Character* (New York: Doubleday, 1992).

West, C., *Race Matters* (New York: Doubleday, 1993).

Wilson, W. J., *The Declining Significance of Race: Blacks and Changing American Institutions* (Chicago: University of Chicago Press, 1980).

Wilson, W. J., "The Black Underclass," *Wilson Quarterly* (1984), pp. 88–99.

Wilson, W. J., *The Truly Disadvantaged: The Inner City, the Underclass, and Public Policy* (Chicago: University of Chicago Press, 1987).

Woodson, R. L. (ed.), *On the Road to Economic Freedom* (Washington, DC: Regnery Gateway, 1987).

Index